# INSECTOPIA:
## *The Wonderful*
## WORLD
## OF INSECTS

Albatros

# Contents

# INTRODUCTION

Insects are, by far, Earth's largest group of multicellular organisms. Currently, we know of over 1 million insect species, meaning they account for over half of the living organisms (animals and plants) we know about. Although we have not yet studied most small insects, some scientists estimate that over 90 percent of all animals are insects. Many entomologists (scientists who study insects) believe that there could be between 6 and 10 million insect species! So in terms of their impact on nature, insects can be considered the most important animal group of all. Insects have settled most of Earth's environments: meadows, forests, streams, steppes, and deserts, to name just a few. They are a rarity only in polar regions and at the tops of the highest mountains. Although they do not live in the sea, they inhabit its surface (think of water striders), while beetle larvae are found in coastal saltwater pools.

Beetles form the largest order of insects and also the largest group of animals on Earth: beetles account for about one-quarter of known species in the kingdom Animalia. There are over 400,000 known beetle species, to which hundreds more—especially in the world's tropical regions—are added each year. The orders Lepidoptera, Hymenoptera, and Diptera all comprise hundreds of thousands of species. All these, plus another 23 insect orders, have a tremendous impact on the terrestrial and freshwater natural environments—the ecosystems of planet Earth. We believe that about 150 million years ago, in the Mesozoic era, insect pollinators sparked the evolution of the flowering plants to which most of today's plant species belong. The existence of many plants is entirely dependent on insects. In the natural world, insects are part of a complex relationship of which pollinating flowers are only one part. They are of crucial importance for the decomposition of organisms and their excrement. The food chains of fish and birds contain billions of individual insects. The insect world has predators and parasites that help nature maintain balance among herbivorous insect species. If we were to go on in this strain, before long we would conclude that most of Earth's ecosystems are directly reliant on insects and that their disappearance would result in the collapse of entire communities of plants and animals.

Insects may be small, but in their relationships between the sexes, their care for their young, their abilities as mimics, and the division of labor in their communities, they have the power to astound us. This book attempts to show all of this. Plus, it seeks to present at least a fraction of the vast miscellany of colors and shapes that makes the insect world not only an exceptionally important part of nature but a beautiful and fascinating one too. We have been entranced by butterfly wings and the metallic elytra (forewing) of beetles for centuries. In the human imagination, however, insects also mean million-strong swarms of locusts and other pests of the field, the calamitous effect wrought by bark beetles on woodland, and serious diseases in humans and animals such as malaria, sleeping sickness, and the Zika virus. On the other hand, we associate summer by the sea with the chirping of cicadas, the flutter of bright-colored butterfly wings, and the buzzing of bees amid fragrant flowers. The reeds of rivers and lakes are vibrant with dragonflies in graceful flight, while twinkling fireflies light up warm summer nights. As well as being both useful and harmful, insects have an effect on human emotions. They are part of our culture, and they are central to our experience of nature.

Some scientists term the epoch we live in today the Anthropocene—the Age of Man. The influence of humans is now present in every place on Earth. Regrettably, the endless growth of civilization is not good for nature, including insects. Although we continue to think of insects as being abundant and ubiquitous, recent scientific findings give cause for concern. Up to 40 percent of insect species face extinction in the next few decades. And that's not all: long-term studies conducted in relatively unspoiled nature reserves in Europe have revealed catastrophic losses of total insect life, in some cases of over 75 percent. The exact cause of this insect apocalypse is unclear, but it is most likely a combination of things including changes in temperature and rainfall, intensive farming using artificial fertilizers and pesticides, the management of extensive forest and field monocultures, and light pollution from public lighting. One reason for the writing of this book was to inspire interest in insects—this marvelous, vital, beautiful, and wide-ranging animal group without which life on our planet would be impossible.

# ANATOMY AND BODY STRUCTURE OF INSECTS

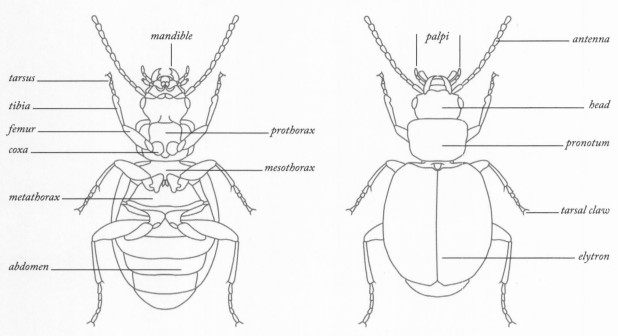

*Morphology of a beetle from below (left) and from above (right)*

Like other arthropods, insects have a visibly segmented body and a hard exoskeleton. The head is formed by the fusion of three original segments, the thorax from three segments, and the abdomen from eleven original segments, some of which fused during evolution. An insect's head has conspicuously segmented antennae containing sensory organs (for smell, taste, and touch, plus temperature and location) and sometimes other functions too. The organs of the mouth develop in accordance with how food is ingested, and they may not be the same in larvae and adults. The large mandibles in the mouthparts of beetles and grasshoppers, for instance, evolved into the piercing/sucking mouthparts of flies, mosquitoes, the sucking mouthparts of butterflies, and the lapping mouthparts of bees.

An insect's eye is a compound of numerous little eyes called ommatidia; in addition, the insect may have the remnants of up to three simple eyes (ocelli). An insect's thorax comprises the prothorax, the mesothorax, and the metathorax, of which each segment has a pair of jointed legs (making a total of six; the subphylum Hexapoda—the largest such insect division—means "six legs" in Greek). Hexapods are easily distinguished from spiders (which have eight legs), centipedes, millipedes, crayfish, and other multi-limbed arthropods. (Each body segment of a primitive arthropod had a pair of limbs that evolved into antennae, mandibles, and palps, or whose growth was stunted.) The mesothorax and the metathorax each have a pair of membranous veined wings, as seen most clearly in the dragonfly. The wings may be interconnected (as in butterflies and hymenopterans), they may be transformed (e.g., the beetle's hard elytra transformed from the first pair of wings), they may have disappeared altogether (as have the wings of the parasitic lice and fleas), or they did not evolve in individuals (as in worker ants and termites). The rear pair of wings of the order Diptera

transformed into small club-shaped organs called halteres, which are used to maintain equilibrium during flight; this explains why flies are such excellent fliers. Insects have no lungs for oxygenating the blood. An insect distributes air through the body via tracheas (tubes that lead through small spiracles in the thorax and abdomen segments), breathing by inflating and deflating the abdomen and thorax. Water beetles do not have gills: they breathe by maintaining an air bubble in the body. As for other aquatic insects, the larvae of mayflies have gills, while those of chironomids take in oxygen with the whole body.

Insect blood is called haemolymph. It isn't red, and it transports only nutrients through the body. Instead of veins, insects have a dorsal vessel, through which, driven by the heart, haemolymph washes through the organs of the body. The abdomen contains a fatty corpuscle that principally serves as a store for energy. An insect's brain is formed by the fusion of several nerve clusters (ganglia), and it resides in the head—although individual ganglia are present in other body segments too, including the abdomen. One of the most immediately interesting things about an insect is its hard exoskeleton, to which muscles and tendons are attached from the inside. This tough shell, known as the cuticle, is composed of a complex glucose known as chitin; in chemical terms, it is close to cellulose in plants. Not only are all body segments, antennae, palps, and limbs reinforced with chitin, but so, too, are reproductive organs (male and female) and insect larvae—although in many cases larvae are softer, their segments less clearly defined, and their antennae very short. This is because larvae are still growing, while adult insects are not. The larvae of some insect orders (notably Diptera) are legless. Butterflies have several pairs of prolegs at the end of the abdomen. The end of a larva's abdomen has several protrusions of various lengths and shapes.

# ORDERS OF INSECTS: A SURVEY

In this chapter, we will familiarize ourselves with the best-known groups of winged insects (Pterygota) and their common and scientific names.

**Dragonflies** (Odonata) are excellent fliers with veined, transparent wings that, when at rest, stand out from the body. They can hover in the air and even fly backwards. Dragonflies are predators. Their enormous eyes almost touch across their faces. Dragonfly larvae catch prey in water, although mostly they do not swim; instead, they lie on the bottom of the water or on plants. They hunt by means of a prehensile organ for grasping prey.

**Stoneflies** (Plecoptera) and **mayflies** (Ephemeroptera) are orders of simple, short-lived insects that live near water; their larvae are aquatic. Adults have long antennae and long paired appendages called cerci at the end of the abdomen. As the wings of the stonefly fold flat over the abdomen, as with most insects, and those of the mayfly fold together over the thorax, it is easy to distinguish the two groups: Palaeoptera (dragonflies and mayflies) and Neoptera (all other orders of winged insects). Neoptera are divided into two groups according to the evolution of their wings as a result of transformation: Exopterygota (which include stoneflies, which undergo an incomplete metamorphosis) and Endopterygota (which undergo a complete metamorphosis).

## EXOPTERYGOTA
*insects that undergo incomplete metamorphosis*

**Earwigs** (Dermaptera) are like rove beetles in that their fan-like wings are hidden under short forewings. Most earwigs do not fly. They have pincers on the abdomen.

**Cockroaches** and **termites** (Blattodea) have a front pair of hardened wings and long antennae. Their long, bristly legs enable them to run fast.

**Mantises** (Mantodea) have small, rotating, triangular heads, folded wings on the back, and bristly forelegs for hunting their prey. An ability to change their color (mimetic coloring) is common.

**Stick insects** (Phasmodea) look like dry twigs or pieces of spined vegetation. They are herbivorous.

**Orthoptera** are divided into two large groups: Ensifera (largely carnivorous crickets with long antennae, as well as herbivorous groups such as mole crickets), and Caelifera (herbivorous grasshoppers with short antennae). Orthoptera fold their wings behind them. They have long legs for jumping. The sound they produce comes from them rubbing together the front pair of wings or the hind femurs. Young Orthoptera look like wingless adults.

**True bugs** (Heteroptera), along with aphids and cicadas, are of the order of Hemiptera. They have piercing-sucking mouthparts, forewings modified to form hemelytra ("half-elytra"), and antennae with only 5 segments. The young are similar to the adults.

The **lice** known as **Psocodea** are small winged or wingless insects with soft bodies. They include parasitic lice.

## ENDOPTERYGOTA (AKA HOLOMETABOLA)
*insects that undergo complete metamorphosis*

The forewings of **beetles** (Coleoptera) are hardened into elytra, under which is a second pair of membranous wings that serve for flight. In exceptional cases (e.g., the rove beetle) the elytra are shortened or the membranous wings are incapable of flight (e.g., larger ground beetles). Hard mandibles allow for carnivorous and herbivorous feeding. Due to the huge number of species, beetles vary greatly in shape, coloring, size, and way of life. The smallest featherwing beetle is only 1 millimeter in length, while the largest longhorn and rhinoceros beetles measure almost 8 inches!

**Snakeflies** (Raphidioptera), **alderflies** (Megaloptera), and **net-winged insects** (Neuroptera) are small orders. Their veined, transparent wings fold roof-like over the body. Many of them have an elongated prothorax. The antlion is a well-known representative of this group.

**Caddisflies** (Trichoptera) are similar to certain moths; however, their wings are folded roof-like. Their larvae live in water and form a protective case.

**Butterflies** (Lepidoptera) are noticeable by their two pairs of wings covered with small scales (in Greek, *lepis* means "scale" and *pteron* means "wing"); the forewings partially cover the hindwings. They suck up nectar from flowers using their long mouthpart, called a proboscis. Butterfly larvae, known as caterpillars, vary in the number of prolegs on the abdomen segment.

**Diptera** (meaning "two wings") have very short antennae and hindwings modified as halteres, which keep them stable in flight. Between the claws, they have spongelike pads that allow them to climb (e.g., on glass). Larvae are legless. Diptera include flies, mosquitoes, and horseflies.

**Hymenoptera** have membranous wings that they fold across the abdomen. The forewings are longer than the hindwings. The hindwings are connected to the forewings by hooks at the edges. Ants have no wings. Some hymenopterans live in communities in which only the queen (e.g., bees, wasps, ants) reproduces, and many of them are parasitic (e.g., sabre wasps). Their larvae are similar to those of the butterflies or are legless.

*Incomplete metamorphosis: development from egg to growing nymph to adult true bug*

As it is with most animals, so it is with insects: the female lays the eggs. The eggs hatch to produce larvae that are not at all similar to adults. Well-known insect larvae include those of the butterfly (caterpillars), the cockchafer, and the aquatic larvae of mosquitos. Larvae pupate, meaning they turn into pupa, which are the immature forms of insects before they become adults. With most orders of insects—including beetles, butterflies, Hymenoptera, and Diptera—a great transformation of tissue, known as complete metamorphosis, occurs in the pupa; what emerges from the pupa is an adult insect fully prepared for the life to come. A few orders develop by incomplete metamorphosis; this means that what hatches from the egg is an adult-like larva, known as a nymph.

Often, this nymph can be distinguished from the adult only by its lack of adult wings and its inability to fly. Nymphs do not end up with a pupa, although they grow and shed one several times. True bugs, grasshoppers, and cockroaches all achieve incomplete metamorphosis, as do mayflies and dragonflies, whose nymphs are adapted for aquatic surroundings, making them very different from adults. There are many exceptions within such a large group of animals, of course. For instance, some insect species do not lay eggs but give birth to larvae or even pupae (e.g., certain flies). Others have no males and their larvae hatch from unfertilized eggs. With social insects such as ants and bees, only the queen reproduces, by laying unfertilized eggs from which, once a season, males emerge capable of fertilizing a new queen during swarming. The new queen saves the male's sperm before laying fertilized eggs that develop into workers. The queen produces a secretion of her own that prevents the workers from reproducing; infertile their whole lives, they remain in the nest. A termite nest has a chamber that contains only the king and queen, whose sole task is to mate. As they develop, termite nymphs become workers or soldiers, as required by the nest. The decisive factor concerning which caste the nymph will assume as an adult remains a mystery. This is probably determined by a combination of food availability and perceptions of smell and touch.

Some insect groups are parasitic. Adult or larval parasites live on (e.g., the adult flea) or inside of (e.g., larval sabre wasp) a host. Common parasites feed on the blood or tissue of the host (e.g., lice in hair or fur). Others develop directly within the host's body. Parasites that eventually kill the host are known as parasitoids. Among insects, notable common parasitoids include larval sabre wasps and various

*Complete metamorphosis: development from egg to larva (caterpillar), pupa, and adult butterfly*

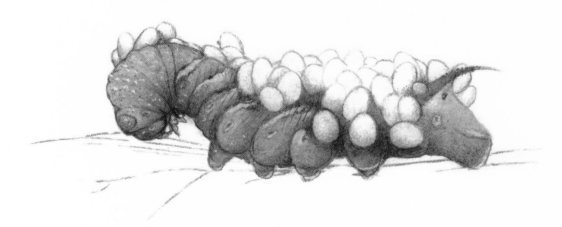

*Caterpillar with pupae of hymenopteran parasite on its body*

other wasps—some of which lay eggs on caterpillars, some of which place their ovipositor inside the victim's body. (The sabre wasp, for instance, lays eggs on larvae living deep in timber.) A larval parasite develops within the body of a caterpillar before drilling itself out through the host's cuticle or pupating in a dead caterpillar. Similarly, larval Diptera (flies and botflies) may develop in the nostrils or under the skin of frogs, ungulates, and other vertebrates, including humans. Nor are so-called hyperparasites (parasites whose hosts are also parasites) uncommon among insects. Notable among hymenopterous insects that engage in multiple parasitism are Braconidae and tiny wasps Chalcidoidea. Wasps of the family Sphecidae hunt spiders and other insects for their larvae, paralyzing them with their sting before carrying them to the nest, where they lay an egg on their paralyzed prey.

Insects living at higher latitudes of the northern and southern hemispheres, and also in the mountains, must be adapted for both cold and warm seasons. Insects reproduce only in the warm season, when but for a few exceptions, all plants grow and flower. Since most insects are short-lived (adults live for a few days, at most a month), the egg or the larvae tend to hibernate. In spring and summer, between one and three generations come into being, the last of which lays eggs (which will hatch in spring) in a concealed place. The cells of species whose larvae live for several years (long-horned beetles can develop in wood for several decades) contain a kind of antifreeze to enable them to survive. Less common, but all the more remarkable for it, is the hibernation of adults (e.g., butterflies) in the attics of houses and crevices in trees. A better-known form of hibernation is practiced by ladybirds, which hatch in the last warm days of autumn before creeping en masse under fallen trees, rocks, and piles of twigs, to be woken there by the spring sun.

The insects best known for their short lives are mayflies, most of which live for only a few days. Many predatory beetles, notably large ground and darkling beetles, live for several years. Larvae or nymphae of insects, including mayflies, often need many years to take on food, shed their old cuticle, and grow. Adults may have stunted mouthparts or take on food in limited amounts, and where this is the case, the main purpose of the male's short life is to find a female with whom to mate. To achieve this, he relies on his excellent sense of smell, whose organ is the antennae, and on many chemical substances—pheromones secreted by females. Insects communicate by a variety of means. Think of fireflies flickering, ants passing information by touching antennae, locusts and crickets chirping, etc.

# EVOLUTION OF INSECTS

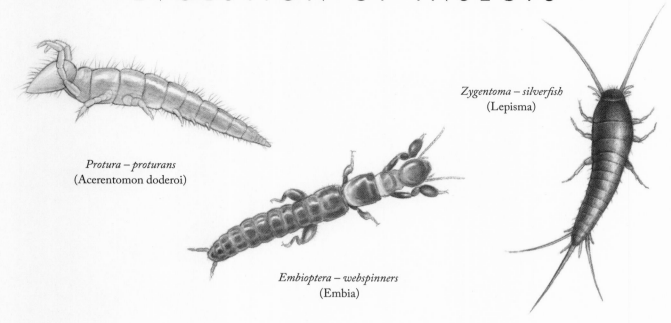

*Protura – proturans*
(Acerentomon doderoi)

*Zygentoma – silverfish*
(Lepisma)

*Embioptera – webspinners*
(Embia)

Insects are arthropods, members of the largest group in the animal kingdom in terms of absolute number and number of species. They are immensely important for the nature of our planet. The latest studies in anatomy, morphology (meaning "body structure"), and genetics show us that insects form the largest and (in terms of evolution) most advanced class of crustaceans, a group that also includes crayfish and crabs. The evolutionary success of insects and the wealth of forms they take can probably be put down to their conquest of the air 300 million years ago, in the early Carboniferous Period, when insects were the only life forms with the ability to fly. This ability has been further developed by different orders of insects over millions of years; as a result, they have succeeded in settling in various environments as many different species.

The relationships between individual insect groups remain a subject of research. In the chapter above on Orders of Insects, we learned about the best-known orders and how to recognize them. Here we will discuss the phylogeny of insects—or the evolutionary relationships between them. To do this, scientists use the so-called phylogenetic tree, formerly known as the evolutionary tree, or simply the tree of life. This is shown on the facing page. The end of each branch of the tree shows one order of insects. The number of pictures behind each branch roughly represents the present number of species of this order (this may have been different in the past). Our tree of life includes only orders of insects that appear in this book (27 in total), none of which are extinct. In the chapters on Paleontology below, we will show many fossils. It is often better to use the scientific names for orders of insects rather than those in common use, since the latter are often confusing or incorrect. Sometimes, we will use both names. For example, Diptera is a scientific name for insects whose most common representatives are flies and mosquitoes. We probably know of Hymenoptera through wasps, bees, and ants; because of their similarity with these, we would be right to assume that bumblebees, sabre wasps, woodwasps, and other small wasps belong in this order.

Entomologists begin with such assumptions as they work out phylogenetic relationships, looking for similarities in body-build and small details on wings and limbs. In recent years, they have been able to identify genetic similarities between objects of study. In the final analysis, they can turn to fossilized traces in rock or ancient amber. From this jigsaw of various pieces of evidence, scientists form hypotheses on insect evolution.

The very term "insect" has two distinct meanings for entomologists. The first is as a broader term to describe the subphylum Hexapoda (Greek for "six legs"), which includes smaller groups of wingless proturans (Protura), "two-pronged bristletails" (Diplura), and springtails (Collembola), which live in terrestrial environments and are rarely longer than 5 mm. On the other hand, the class Insecta (otherwise known as Ectognatha) also has wingless representatives, the best known of which include the silverfish in our bathroom (they are of the order Zygentoma). Some insects have wings, while others have lost them secondarily. The most primitive insects are Palaeoptera (dragonflies and mayflies), whose wings fold over the thorax or are held away from the body. Other insects (Neoptera) can fold the wings over the abdomen, either roof-like or flat. Members of the same order do not always look alike, as they may have adapted to extreme living conditions in the course of evolution. Termites are of the same order as cockroaches, although they are adapted for social life in dark nests, divided into castes. Fleas are wingless creatures adapted for life in the extreme conditions of animal fur; they are very unlike scorpionflies, from which they evolved. In evolutionary terms, the most advanced superorder of insects is Holometabola (also known as Endopterygota), which undergoes a complete metamorphosis. Also the largest insect phylogenetic lineage, it includes beetles, butterflies, Hymenoptera, Diptera, and several less numerous orders. They are distinguished from other insects by their larval form (which does not resemble the adult) and the pupa, the stage at which the larva transforms into the adult.

# EVOLUTIONARY TREE OF INSECTS

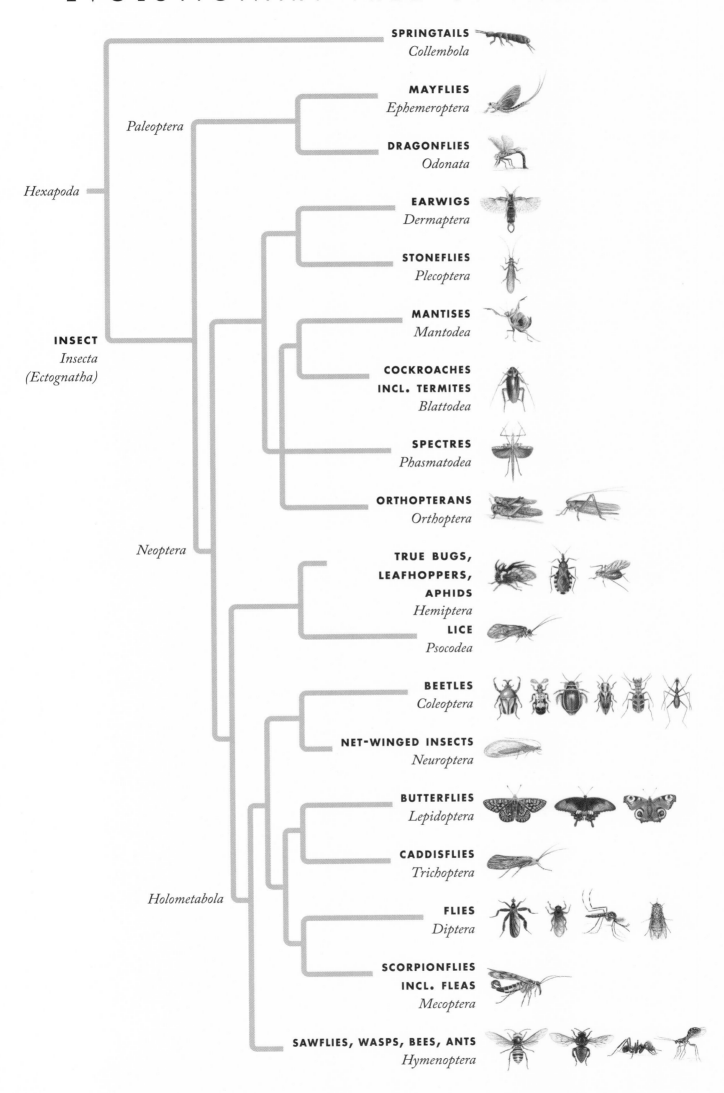

**SPRINGTAILS**
*Collembola*

**MAYFLIES**
*Ephemeroptera*

**DRAGONFLIES**
*Odonata*

**EARWIGS**
*Dermaptera*

**STONEFLIES**
*Plecoptera*

**MANTISES**
*Mantodea*

**COCKROACHES INCL. TERMITES**
*Blattodea*

**SPECTRES**
*Phasmatodea*

**ORTHOPTERANS**
*Orthoptera*

**TRUE BUGS, LEAFHOPPERS, APHIDS**
*Hemiptera*

**LICE**
*Psocodea*

**BEETLES**
*Coleoptera*

**NET-WINGED INSECTS**
*Neuroptera*

**BUTTERFLIES**
*Lepidoptera*

**CADDISFLIES**
*Trichoptera*

**FLIES**
*Diptera*

**SCORPIONFLIES INCL. FLEAS**
*Mecoptera*

**SAWFLIES, WASPS, BEES, ANTS**
*Hymenoptera*

*Hexapoda*

*Paleoptera*

**INSECT**
*Insecta*
*(Ectognatha)*

*Neoptera*

*Holometabola*

# DAWN OF THE INSECTS

## *The Devonian, the Carboniferous, the Permian*

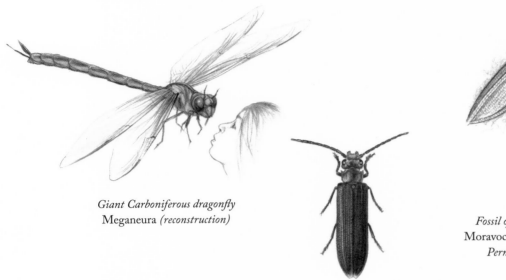

Giant Carboniferous dragonfly
Meganeura *(reconstruction)*

*Fossil of the oldest known beetle*
Moravocoleus permianus, *found in*
*Permian strata in Czechia*

Cupes mucidus, *a present-day representative of the ancient*
*family Cupedidae, related to beetles of the Permian*

The oldest known animal fossil of insect-like creature originates from the Devonian Period of the Palaeozoic Era. We estimate its age at 410 million years. It was discovered in 1919, in a field of chert (a type of quartz rock) near the small Scottish village of Rhynie—hence the name *Rhyniella praecursor* (a precursor is a forerunner or ancestor). Paleontologists believe it to be a springtail (Collembola), which is a member of Hexapoda. It is very closely related to the insects of today. Some scientists believe that the mouthparts of *Rhyniella praecursor* are in fact those of another fossil, which was later given the name *Rhyniognatha hirsti*. Opinions differ as to how Rhyniognatha should be classified. Some paleontologists believe that it had wings and was related to the mayfly; others believe it was related to the centipede, which has little in common with insects. As the case may be, we know for sure that it was in the Devonian Period that terrestrial animal and plant life forms came into being, and these include arthropods.

The fossils we have from the Carboniferous Period (from 359 million to 299 million years ago) have far clearer features. In this period, Earth was first covered with plants—mainly tree-like club mosses (lycophytes) up to 100 feet tall, horsetails, and ferns. Later, seedless plants, including conifers, appeared. With their warm climate, the vast primeval forests of the Carboniferous Period provided a perfect environment for insects to develop in. This time period saw the origination of many insect orders that are with us to this day. Insects became planet Earth's first flyers. The oldest flying insects are mayflies and dragonflies, whose nymphs lived aquatically in vast swamps. Predatory dragonflies ruled the skies, and they grew to incredible proportions—the best known of them, Meganeura, had a wingspan of up to two and a half feet! Insects of the Carboniferous were probably so large because conditions favored them; they had no competitors in the skies.

One order of insects that has not survived to the present day is Palaeodictyoptera. It became extinct at the end of the Permian Period. Palaeodictyoptera, too, grew to estimable proportions; Mazothairos, for instance, had a wingspan of nearly two feet, as well as a mighty body and long appendages on the trunk. The *Dunbaria fasciipennis* fossil, discovered in Kansas, features beautifully speckled wings. Palaeodictyoptera probably had aquatic nymphs, and the adults fed by sucking on plants. More interesting still, they are the only animal in history to have six wings—a pair on each segment of the thorax. The wings of the prothorax were small and rounded, and we don't know what they were used for.

Other insect orders, too, originated in the Carboniferous and Permian Periods. The Carboniferous gave us fossils of cockroaches and the ancestors of crickets, grasshoppers, and stoneflies. Diversification of insects occurred in the Permian, 250 to 300 million years ago. From this period, we have the beautiful fossils of many insect orders that underwent incomplete metamorphosis, as well as the earliest examples of orders that underwent complete metamorphosis. These include Permian beetles, which have remained practically unchanged to the present day. The suborder Archostemata occurred all over the world in the Permian Period; that it exists today is remarkable. In the past, its larvae probably developed as they do today, in the wood of conifers. As the Permian gave way to the Triassic Period, 252 million years ago, huge volcanic eruptions resulted in a mass extinction event known as the Great Dying, in which 90 percent of the world's animal species perished. Insects were affected by this disaster, but they survived.

« *The palaeodictyoptera* Stenodictya *(foreground) and the dragonfly* Meganeura *(above). The cockroach on the horsetail stalk resembles today's species.*

# DIVERSIFICATION OF INSECTS

## *The Triassic to the Cenozoic*

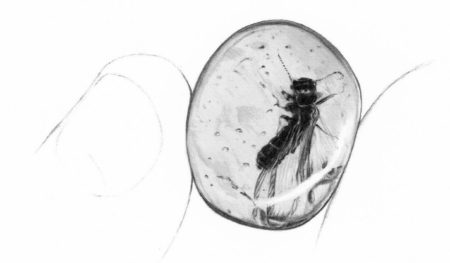

*Many fossils from the Middle Jurassic Period have been found in the sediment of freshwater lakes.* Sinomelyris praedecessor *from China was described in 2019.*

*Extraordinarily well-preserved insect fossils, such as this winged termite, have been found in Burmese amber almost 100 million years old*

The Great Dying marked the beginning of the Mesozoic Era and the Triassic Period, from which very few fossilized insects have been discovered. It is probable that many of the insect families we know today, such as the rove beetle (Staphylinidae), originated soon after the world recovered. Even so, the end of the Triassic (201 million years ago) brought another mass extinction event, for reasons unknown. This explains why insect life did not properly develop until the following period, the Jurassic, which has provided us with some beautifully preserved fossils, notably from Australia, China, and Siberia. The first gymnosperms pollinated by insects originated in the Jurassic, about 160 million years ago. These include cycads, which still grow today, pollinated by small beetles whose lineage can be tracked back all the way to the mid-Jurassic, 165 million years ago. The large picture shows us what things may have looked like at that time. Many fossils of beetles with long mandibles (of the extinct family Parandrexidae) have been discovered in geological strata of the Jurassic and Cretaceous Periods in China, southern Siberia, and Spain.

Fossils from the Jurassic Period teach us about most insect orders and many insect families that are with us today. These include true bugs, cicadas, and many beetles well preserved because of their tough cuticles. Many fossils are found in sediment of former freshwater lakes and sites of temporary pools into which flying insects fell and where they were covered by the mud of ages, fossilizing over many years into fine-grained shale. Sometimes, sediment turns up groups of insects that surprise us, such as enormous fleas that probably sucked the blood of dinosaurs.

The Cretaceous Period witnessed the rapid development of angiosperms: plants that bear flowers and fruits. Along with these plants, insects developed to assume the role of pollinator in exchange for the flowers' sweet nectar. Of the many insect species that emerged at this time, some fed on the sap of plants, while others fed on leaves, stalks, and roots. The origination of herbivorous insects was followed closely by the evolution of their parasites and predators. This is the time of the origination of many beautiful fossils preserved in shale, as well as in amber (fossilized tree resin). Cretaceous amber has been discovered in Western Europe, the Middle East, eastern parts of North America, and most notably, in Myanmar. This is how we know about the lives of insects 100 million years ago, when dinosaurs ruled the Earth.

The Cenozoic Era followed the last mass extinction event, which occurred 66 million years ago. It gave us the vast majority of insect orders and families still with us today. It is plain that insects were far better equipped to survive the collision of an asteroid with Earth than dinosaurs and pterosaurs. The warm damp climate of the early Cenozoic was good for insects and plants, and their coevolution resulted in a great richness of species and ways of life. Huge colonies of social insects and herbivores, together with their parasites and predators, resulted in so many insects that in terms of both species and individuals, insects were far greater in number than any other animal group. The Era of the Insect had begun.

« *Beetles of the extinct family Parandrexidae were the first pollinators of cycads. We have fossils of them from Mesozoic Europe and Asia.*

# COURTSHIP AND NUPTIAL GIFTS

## *Dance flies (Diptera: Hybotidae, Empididae)*

*North American dance flies in flight at sunset*

Rhamphomyia longicauda *female*

Rhamphomyia longicauda *male*

We encounter dance flies (aka dagger flies, balloon flies) from April to August, in open landscapes on the edge of woodland, meadows, and clearings. This unusual family of dipterans performs remarkable courtship rituals. At first glance, dance flies could be mistaken for more ordinary long-bodied flies. They tend to be between 10 and 15 mm long. They sit on flower clusters such as angelica, ground elder, and carrot, where they feed on nectar. Males and larvae are predatory, hunting other insects of comparable size—males in flight, larvae in litter or under fallen leaves.

In the courting season, the male hunts other flies and insects, which he brings to the female as a nuptial gift. The female does not hunt, and as such is entirely dependent on the male to survive, since the little nectar she takes from flowers provides her only with sugar, not protein. Our picture shows the dance fly *Empis tessellata*, which is about 10 mm long and can be found over a wide area, from Europe to Japan. The male has presented the female with his gift, a black-and-red froghopper (*Cercopis vulnerata*), and she is chowing down. Hanging from a leaf by his front legs, he uses his other two pairs to hold the female and couple with her as she feasts. In the background, another

male is holding a fly he has caught, presenting it to a female. For courtship, dance flies often come together in a swarm, with males trying to attract females. A female chooses the suitor who brings the largest or most alluring gift.

Among the 3,000-plus species of dance flies are some among which swarms are formed by males in competition with each other for the attention of watching females. There are also species in which females form swarms to attract males. The females of the North American long-tailed dance fly (*Rhamphomyia longicauda*) form swarms of up to 100 individuals at sunset. Males attempt to attract swarming females with tasty morsels and also with their appearance; their middle and hind legs have long pinnate scales, and they have dark wings. By inflating their pleural sacs, they make themselves look bigger and more striking.

The male of some species presents an even better nuptial gift. He packs insects he has caught in a cocoon of silk fiber which he has woven himself. When presented with such a gift, the female does not unpack it; instead, she pierces the cocoon with her proboscis, which she uses to suck out the prey. Did someone say that the way to a girl's heart is through her stomach?

« *The courtship of* Empis tessellata *dance flies takes place on the edge of woodland, where the male presents his nuptial gift.*

# ADAPTING TO ISLAND LIFE
## Weta (Orthoptera: Ensifera)

*Male weta*
(Hemideina crassidens)

*Enemies of weta include
the Polynesian rat*
(Rattus exulans), *a rat
brought to islands by humans*

New Zealand is the home of many plants and animals that are found nowhere else in the world. Such plants and animals are known as endemic species or groups. New Zealand's endemites include flightless crickets, referred to by the Māori word *weta*, a collective name comprising almost 70 species of two families of Orthoptera ("straight wings"). Weta are wingless or have stunted wings, making them incapable of flight. Otherwise, they are similar to more widespread cricket and grasshopper species. A female weta of the *Deinacrida heteracantha* species has been known to weigh 2.5 ounces. Only the Goliath flower chafers of Africa can compete with that! The giant weta of the genus *Deinacrida* are up to four inches long. They live near the coasts of the islands and in the mountains of New Zealand's South Island. Some are among the heaviest insects in the world. These creatures are an example of the biological phenomenon known as insular gigantism. Isolated on an island with no natural enemies, some species grow to be much larger than their mainland relatives. This is the case not only with weta, but also with giant Polynesian snails, Madagascan and New Zealand flightless birds, giant turtles on the Galápagos Islands, and many others. Conversely, large animal species transferred to a small island may become smaller over time, most likely because the island cannot feed a larger animal. This phenomenon is known as insular dwarfism. We're thinking of extinct elephants and mammoths of the islands of the Mediterranean, whose skulls gave rise to the myths of the Cyclops.

Weta are nocturnal creatures. During the day, they rest in fallen leaves, under tree bark, or in crevices in rock. Some species live in caves. Smaller species tend to be carnivorous, while most larger ones are herbivorous. Like other crickets and grasshoppers, weta stridulate, or chirp. This sound is made by the rubbing of hind legs against a tough, ridged plate on the side of the abdomen. As with other crickets, stridulation serves the male for the defense of his gallery against competing males, communication between the sexes, and warning in the face of danger. Some weta of

the genus *Hemideina* live in trees: in galleries formed by large beetles. Here, the male lives with a harem of up to 10 females. Some locals find the chirping of weta so pleasing that they drill holes in pieces of wood for them to settle in. Other Hemideina species live in solitude; in the mating season, the male brings the female a nuptial gift of something good to eat. With some species, the female stays in an underground chamber with her clutch of eggs, caring for them until they hatch—behavior that's unusual among orthopterans.

Mountain species of weta, notably *Hemideina maori* and *Deinacrida connectens*, are unusual for their ability to withstand variations in temperature. In winter, they are frozen and immobile for up to five months, covered in ice crystals with their biological functions suspended. Hibernation of hidden larvae and adults is no rarity among insects. Perhaps none, however, undergo such a prolonged freeze and crystallization of water in tissue as weta. Not only do weta not take refuge from the cold before their lengthy hibernation, but they can also withstand nighttime mountain frosts. They thaw out each morning before refreezing each evening.

Before the arrival of people in New Zealand about 1,000 years ago, weta had only a handful of natural enemies. In addition to bats and kiwi birds, these included the tuatara (*Sphenodon punctatus*), the last survivor of an ancient order of reptiles with a "third eye" on top of the head, which now lives near the coast of only a few islands. In the picture, we see the *Deinacrida heteracantha* and a tuatara on the edge of a forest. Both creatures are slow-moving, so the hunt appears to play out in slow motion.

In addition to their natural predators, weta have become threatened by mammals brought to their surroundings by people. In New Zealand, these include the hedgehog, the Polynesian rat, cats, and weasels, for all of whom weta are easy prey. As a result, it is no surprise that the giant *Deinacrida*, along with a third of other weta species, are threatened with extinction and so are on the endangered species list.

« *Weta are hunted by another "living fossil"—the tuatara.*

# FIGHTING FOR THE FEMALE

*European stag beetle – Lucanus cervus (Coleoptera: Lucanidae)*

*Male European
stag beetle in flight*

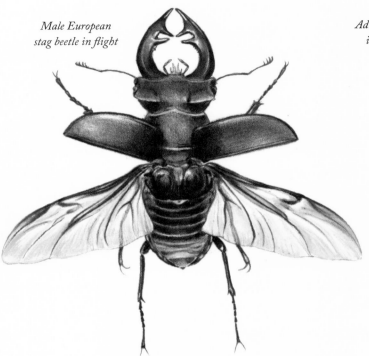

*Adult stag beetle larva
in typical position*

*In the wild, the pupa of the stag beetle is well hidden
in a solid cocoon; in the picture, it is exposed*

Ritualistic or real fights between males for the right to produce offspring with a female occur throughout the animal kingdom. Among the best known duels are between stags, walruses, and ruffs. The female watches the contest before mating with the best-performing male. It is very common for parts of the male body used in such a fight (e.g., the stag's antlers) to be oversized. This is the case with insects too. Fights between longhorn beetles and rhinoceros beetles, which push their heads against each other, are among the best known. Better known still are fights between stag beetles. The male stag beetle has extraordinarily large mandibles, which do battle for the favor of the female. The family *Lucanidae*, which occurs all over the world, has over 1,200 species, the largest of which are up to nearly 5 inches long. The mandibles of the male have a remarkable, distinctive shape. The mandibles of some stag beetles (e.g., the magnificent metallic green *Lamprima adolphinae* species from New Guinea) point upwards at an angle. As the female does not have oversized mandibles, the sexes can be told apart with ease. This phenomenon is known as sexual dimorphism.

The European stag beetle is Europe's biggest beetle, with mandibles up to 3.5 inches long. Its scientific name, *Lucanus cervus*, is a clear reference to its "antlers"; *cervus* means "stag" in Latin. Although the female stag beetle is much smaller than the male, the pressure applied by her short sharp mandibles tends to be greater. Stag beetles live in deciduous woodland. Females lay their eggs in dying oak branches and stumps, and it is there that their larvae—blind and white, like the grubs of the cockchafer—develop. Stag beetle larvae may develop in the wood of other deciduous trees too, such as beech, willow, ash, and fruit-bearing trees.

They stridulate using combs in their legs, thus communicating with other larvae in the area. After about three years of development, larvae pupate in a dark, egg-like cocoon containing tiny pieces of wood and earth. It was discovered only recently that when approaching completion of their development, in early spring, larvae may crawl into the earth below the place of their development, to remain there for the next two or three months to complete their development and pupate. Adult beetles emerge from their cocoons at the end of spring, after which they live for just a few weeks. In this time, they feed only on sweet fruit juices or the sap of damaged trees. As spring turns into summer, on warm evenings male stag beetles fly to thick branches and tree trunks, where they settle. There they get into fights, with each duelist grabbing the mandibles of the other in an attempt to knock him from the tree. With the fight over, the victor hurries to be with the female of his choice, who is waiting for him nearby. This explains why we sometimes come across males with damaged elytra. Such duels do not result in serious injury or death, however.

Because of their size, stag beetles have no insect enemies, but they are at risk of being eaten by bats, foxes, and many bird species. Meanwhile, their fat, helpless larvae are very attractive to hungry woodpeckers. Unfortunately for stag beetles, modern forestry does them no favors by clearing away old and decaying wood, and the mighty stumps of deciduous trees are becoming increasingly rare. Environments in which stag-beetle larvae can develop are ever fewer. This fate is shared by many other insect species dependent on mighty old trees, which are disappearing as dense human populations take over the landscape.

« *Male European stag beetles in combat, each trying to grasp the mandibles of the other and knock him from the tree. A female stands by waiting for the victor.*

# FLYING ACROBATS

## *Dragonflies (Odonata)*

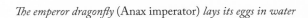

*The emperor dragonfly* (Anax imperator) *lays its eggs in water*

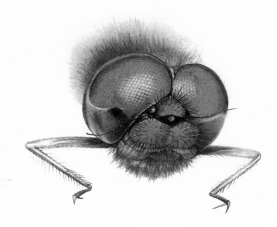

*A dragonfly's eyes are so large that in some species they touch on the top of the head*

Dragonflies have brought life to the shores of freshwater pools, rivers, and lakes for an incredible 300 million years. As they maneuver above the water in search of insects, defend their territory, reproduce, and lay their eggs, all with wonderful agility, they remind us of little helicopters or drones. They can fly straight up and down, hover, and even fly backwards. They achieve all this by rapidly beating their large wings (up to 30 beats per second), and by beating their forewings and hindwings independently of each other. In addition, thanks to their huge compound eyes, which occupy most of the surface of the head, dragonflies have excellent eyesight. This allows them to see their prey from several yards away. Between a pair of eyes comprising up to 28,000 facets are three simple eyes for perceiving light.

Today's world contains about 6,000 dragonfly species. All hold their wings away from the body; they are unable to fold them along the abdomen. This makes them easy for us to identify. Large dragonfly species are over 4 inches long, with a wingspan of up to 8 inches.

With a few exceptions, dragonfly larvae live in water. As they undergo incomplete metamorphosis, we refer to them as nymphs. Like adults, they are predatory. They spend their days on the stems of aquatic plants. They swim short distances with the help of three little fins near the end of the abdomen, or by jet propulsion—they shoot forward by ejecting a swift stream of water from the abdomen. Another peculiarity of the dragonfly nymph is the prehensile organ for grasping prey, which is adapted from the mouthparts. The nymph shoots this rapidly forward to a distance of a third of its body length. In this way, it hunts other aquatic insects or tiny amphibian tadpoles. In a life lasting several years, the nymph moults (i.e., sheds its skin) at least 10 times. At the end of the development process, usually on a summer morning, the nymph emerges from the water by clinging to a stone or the stalk of a plant. Then it moults for the last time. After that, the adult dragonfly emerges from its exuvia—the remains of its exoskeleton. It pumps air into its body through the veins in its wings and allows its exoskeleton to harden. We may come across the exuvia in waterside reeds.

Dragonflies have a remarkable way of mating. The male has two copulating organs: one at the end of the abdomen, where sperm are formed, as with other insects, plus secondary genitalia at the front of the long abdomen, to which sperm are transferred by curling the abdomen. Often in flight, the male grasps the female's head with the pincers at the end of his abdomen; so that he may fertilize her eggs, the female curls her abdomen to pick up sperm from his secondary genitalia. The couple then forms a flying "heart" posture, in the air or on leaves. How charmingly simple!

« *A pair of common blue damselflies* (Enallagma cyathigerum) *and a scarlet dragonfly* (Crocothemis erythraea). *Attached to the reeds is the exuvia of a dragonfly nymph that has come from the water and transformed into an adult.*

# THE SHORT LIFE OF THE MAYFLY

## *Mayflies (Ephemeroptera)*

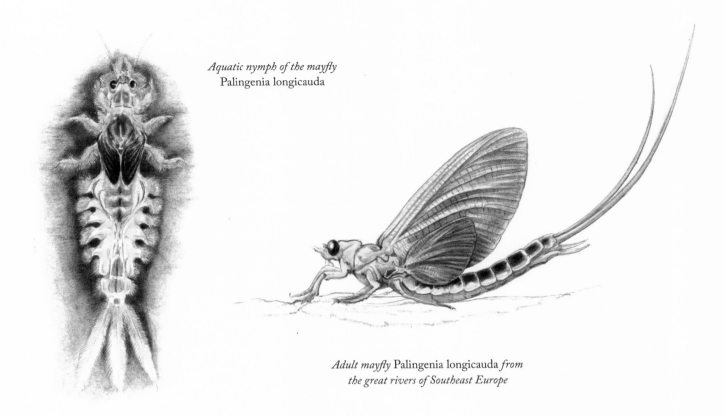

*Aquatic nymph of the mayfly*
Palingenia longicauda

*Adult mayfly* Palingenia longicauda *from
the great rivers of Southeast Europe*

Mayflies are synonymous with the shortness of life. According to common wisdom, a mayfly's life is dedicated to producing the next generation—and nothing more. Nature puts everything in its right place, however; every living creature is part of a complex ecosystem of plants and animals. Adult mayflies are very short-lived indeed. Found in vast swarms, they provide food for fish, birds, and insectivorous mammals, including very large creatures such as the American black bear. Mayfly nymphs are found en masse on the muddy bottoms of slow rivers, there forming an important part of the diet of creatures that share their habitat. In mountain streams, the presence of mayfly nymphs is an indicator of water purity.

Along with the dragonfly, the mayfly belongs to the ancestral group *Palaeoptera*, which first inhabited our planet in the Paleozoic Era. It folds its wings over the thorax only. Like the dragonfly, it undergoes incomplete metamorphosis, and its nymphs are aquatic. They feed on small aquatic organisms and detritus (decayed organic matter). As they grow, mayfly nymphs moult several times, over several months, perhaps even years. They come ashore at last to transform into winged larvae, and from that into adult mayflies. The mouthparts and digestive tract of a mayfly are stunted, and as a result it is unable to feed. Males congregate in swarms above or near water. Females fly to these swarms for mating to take place in the air. Impregnated females go on to drop their eggs on the water, or else they dive in and deposit eggs in clusters on rocks and plants.

Mayfly species afraid of the lazy flow of great rivers often come together in huge numbers. Perhaps the best known of such mayfly swarms—of the genus *Hexagenia*, principally *Hexagenia bilineata*—occur at the upper and middle Mississippi River, most notably in the state of Iowa. An early-evening mayfly swarm may obscure the sky, resembling a great storm cloud. When this phenomenon occurs, doors and windows must be closed, while traffic comes to a stop as mayflies cover the road surface, the cars on it, trees, and everything else in the neighborhood. The mayflies are attracted by street lighting, which naturally they also cover. In Europe, the giant mayfly *Palingenia longicauda* forms vast swarms over the River Tisza in Hungary, Serbia, and Slovakia, where for a few days in mid-June they become a tourist attraction. These creatures measure between 5 and 10 inches from head to tail! Rather than flying free, they circle above the river, often drawing their long hair-like setae across its surface. The "Tisza Blossom"—as this swarming is known—occurs in daylight too, when males do everything in their power to mate in the few hours of life available to them. The females lay their eggs on the river; when they die soon thereafter, they have provided for new life below the surface. And so the cycle of swarming and death is repeated year after year.

« Palingenia longicauda *mayflies spend their short life on the surface of a river. They mate in riparian vegetation and lay their eggs on the water when in flight.*

# INSECT STATES
## *Termites (Blattodea: Isoptera)*

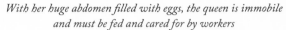

*With her huge abdomen filled with eggs, the queen is immobile and must be fed and cared for by workers*

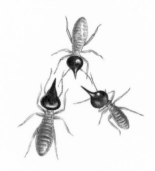

*The soldier caste of the subfamily* Nasutitermitinae, *whose mandibles have evolved into sprayers*

It may be difficult to believe, but termites are eusocial Insects (meaning they live in cooperative groups) that belong to the same order as cockroaches—one of the oldest insect orders in evolutionary terms, which emerged in the early Carboniferous Period. Fossil finds tell us that cockroaches have lived on our planet in practically unchanged form for 350 million years. Sometime in the Mesozoic Era—most likely in the Jurassic Age, over 150 million years ago—one evolutionary line of cockroaches discovered a way of life in large colonies, with division of labor among socially adapted groups of individuals known as castes. In this way, termites emerged.

We tend to associate termites with wood-eating. Termites do, of course, eat wood, but what is less well known is that most modern-day termite species feed on organic matter in the soil. All termites live in symbiosis with organisms that help them break down difficult-to-digest cellulose, including wood. This clears the way for protozoa living in the gut, as well as fungus, which termites cultivate in gardens inside nests. About 50 million years ago, some termites replaced protozoa in the gut with bacteria, facilitating a change in diet from wood to organic matter in soil. Today, this is the diet of 2,400 of the 3,000 termite species.

The nest contains a king and a queen in a walled chamber to which only workers have access. Workers care for the royal couple, especially the queen, by feeding and cleaning them and taking away the eggs the queen has laid. The king fertilizes the queen inside the chamber. Both king and queen have lost their wings. The queen is now large, immobile, and perhaps over 4 inches long. Termite nymphs of both sexes hatch from her eggs. Their caste will be determined by food and odor and touch sensation, which develop in contact with other nymphs and adults. The most numerous caste in the nest comprises the workers, of which there may be over a million. They have a soft body, atrophied eyes, and they cannot reproduce. Workers provide food for the entire colony, build and repair the nest, cultivate symbiotic fungus, maintain tunnels for transport-

ing food, manage ventilation in the nest or mound, and perform many other tasks. The only task of the soldier termite is defense of the nest. Most soldiers are blind and wingless, with atrophied genitals. Unlike the worker, the soldier has a large, hard head with large mandibles, or—as is the case with the nasute termites (*Nasutitermes*) of South America, which defend against the predatory anteater—a head that can stretch into a nozzle, with which it sprays an attacker with a stinking, sticky liquid. Enemies of termites include some ants, although certain other ant species share a nest with termites. Relationships in nature can be quite complicated, can't they?

Termite mounds are among the largest structures in the animal kingdom; they can be up to 16 feet high and 65 feet in diameter. They are built of various materials, most notably particles of soil bound together by saliva to form a remarkable fortress. Some termites live in underground nests and trees. As all termites shy away from light, they build tunnels leading out of the nest to store food in. Some of these tunnels are underground. Other tunnels are made of soil at the ground level and enclosed; still others are made in tree trunks or branches. Ground-level termite mounds are a common sight on sun-drenched savannas. In such a sun-heated structure, it is difficult to keep temperature and humidity at tolerable levels. *Amitermes meridonialis*, an Australian termite, is commonly known as the magnetic termite or the compass termite, because of its interesting solution to this problem. Its flat mound is up to 13 feet tall and aligned so that the main axis runs north and south. As a result, its eastern and western sides receive the warmth of the sun in the morning and evening respectively, giving each time to cool. Only its narrow top surface is exposed to the scorching midday sun. The temperature in the mound should never exceed 95° Fahrenheit; if it does, the termites inside die. The chamber of the king and queen is in an underground part of the mound, where the temperature is mildest. After all, nothing is more valuable to the colony than its queen.

« *Australian termites* (Amitermes) *build their mounds with reference to magnetic force. In the foreground we see two winged individuals during swarming.*

# SLAVE-MAKERS, SLAVES, AND WARRIORS

## Ants (Hymenoptera: Formicidae)

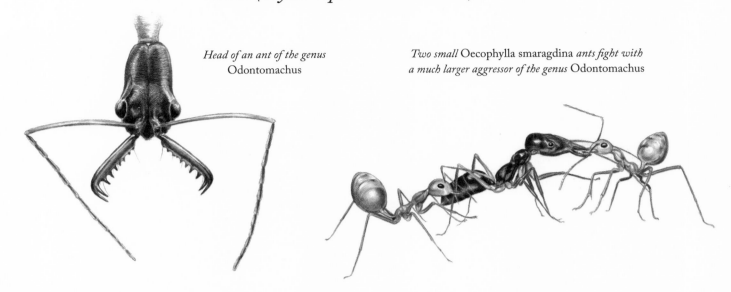

*Head of an ant of the genus* Odontomachus

*Two small* Oecophylla smaragdina *ants fight with a much larger aggressor of the genus* Odontomachus

According to the famous biologist E. O. Wilson, ants are without a doubt the most aggressive and combative of all animals: if they had nuclear weapons at their disposal, they would end the world in a single day. The conflict between the North American *Pheidole dentata* (big-headed) ant and the "red fire" ant *Solenopsis invicta* (spread to many parts of the world from South America) is a good example of an interspecies war. The latter got its nickname from the powerful poison in its sting and its notorious aggressiveness. The domestic *Pheidole dentata* has developed an ingenious tactic for the struggle against an invader. When the worker Pheidole comes across the Solenopsis, rather than fight, it seeks to make contact with the adversary's body so as to capture its odor and take it back to its nest. It marks its way back with a secretion from its olfactory glands, thus alerting all ants of its own species. Its return to the nest results in mass mobilization: workers and soldiers set out along the odor trail in pursuit of the enemy.

When the two species meet, a battle at last begins, although some workers drenched in the odor of the Solenopsis return to their nest to gather reinforcements for the fight. The number of Pheidole ants on the battlefield grows and grows even before the soldiers join the fray. Unlike workers, soldiers do not use their sting; instead, they use their powerful mandibles to sever limbs and abdomen segments from the bodies of the larger Solenopsis. After the battle, workers and soldiers patrol the area to make sure that the last intruder has been killed: no enemy should be allowed to return to its nest and testify to the presence of a nearby Pheidole colony, since the Pheidole nest could not resist an all-out Solenopsis attack. If such a thing does happen, Pheidole soldiers form a line around the entrance in an attempt to stop the Solenopsis from getting in. Having thus bought themselves time, they will

then fight to the last breath. Meanwhile, the workers grab the larvae, eggs, and pupae before attempting to break through the front and find a hiding place. Even the queen tries to flee. After the invaders have plundered the anthill, the workers return. If the queen, too, succeeds in making it back, the nest will recover from the attack.

The relationship between slave-making ants and enslaved ants is a strange one. At the end of spring, arrays of raiding worker ants of the slave-making species *Polyergus rufescens*, commonly referred to as the Amazon ant, search the nests of other ants, notably the woodland *Formica* genus. Their aim is to steal a pupa or a large larva from some strangers' nest before taking it to their own nest. Indeed, the Amazon queen originally established their nest in the anthill of strangers – by killing their queen, then taking over her workers. The workers of the original queen continue to serve the nest, together with its new queen. To ensure that these enslaved workers live on without their own procreating queen, the slave-making Amazons return from their raids of other nests with larvae and pupae to become enslaved Formica workers.

Our scene shows tiny North American ants called *Temnothorax pilagens*, which, in commandos of about four members, search the nests (found in hollowed nuts or acorns) of related species *T. longispinosus* and *T. ambiguus*. Fortified and guarded against larger invaders, these have only one narrow entrance. One of the commandos, the scout, leads its companions to the nest. By means of chemical camouflage, they sneak inside and bear away the larvae without raising the suspicions of the nest's defenders. Sometimes they even take adult prisoners, who will go on to manage operations in the slavers' nest. By not killing the worker ants they attack, aggressor ants can raid a neighboring nest and enslave its inhabitants repeatedly.

« *A slave-raiding commando of* Temnothorax pilagens *ants prepares to penetrate the nest of* Temnothorax ambiguus *ants in a hazelnut.*

# COURTSHIP IN THE HILLS

*Fritillaries, browns, swallowtails (Lepidoptera: Nymphalidae, Papilionidae)*

*Marsh fritillary* (Eurodryas aurina)

*Large wall brown* (Lasiommata maera)

*A marsh fritillary at rest shows off the different colors of the underside of its wings*

On bare hilltops in spring and summer, we often encounter swarms of flies, winged ants, wasps, and other hymenopterans, as well an abundance of lovely butterflies. The remarkable phenomenon is known as "hilltopping."

Insects seek out the tops of tall hills where growth is sparse. If they must, they will make do with a small ridge on a plain, a tree overhanging its group, or even a solitary but distinctive rock. In an industrial area they tend to settle on excavation heaps. In these prominent places, males and females rendezvous in the search of a mate. European butterflies known for their hilltopping include swallowtails, browns, pierids, gossamer-winged butterflies, and fritillaries. For days, male butterflies fly around a bare hilltop, competing with one another to capture the best (i.e., most visible) places, which are usually at the very top. Females fly there to choose a male occupying one of these places, since in genetic terms these males are probably the strongest and fittest. This explains why there tend to be more males than females on hilltops. Of the females that are there, almost none are already fertilized. There is a special case in tropical Africa, where males of the butterfly genus *Acraea* are commonly infected by Wolbachia bacteria. As a result,

its males are so scarce on hilltops that the females must compete for them.

Large numbers of flying insects on hilltops attract insectivorous birds, such as swallows and swifts, as well as insect predators like dragonflies, dipterous flies, and other predatory insects that hunt in flight.

This picture shows a Southern European landscape with a hilltop covered with only grass and scrub. The insects in flight competing for the hill's highest point and marking out their small territories are males of the common yellow swallowtail (*Papilio machaon*). The females on the blades of grass in the foreground will choose the fittest males to become fathers to their caterpillars. These will feed on leaves of flower clusters (e.g., carrot, fennel, burnet, dill) for several weeks before pupating; a week or two after this, a new butterfly will emerge from the pupa. The speed of a swallowtail's development depends on the temperature; in colder regions such as Alaska, Siberia, and the Himalayas, only one generation will emerge each spring/ summer, while in the warmer climes of Europe, Asia, and North America, the same period will produce up to three generations of these lovely creatures.

« *An old world swallowtail* (Papilio machaon) *during hilltopping. The resting female will choose from the males flying around.*

# LIFE IN DARKNESS

*Ground beetles (Carabidae) and round fungus beetles (Leiodidae)*

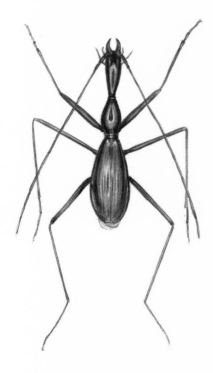

*The wingless, blind ground beetle* Dongodytes tonywhitteni *from South China*

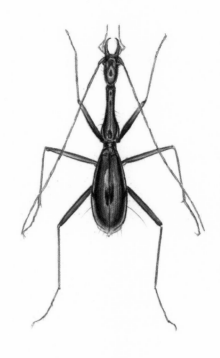

*The ground beetle* Xuedytes bellus *from South China has asymmetrical mandibles*

In this chapter, we travel to a damp, cold, subterranean world, home to strange blind, wingless creatures known as troglobionts. Troglofauna are cave-dwelling animals that spend their whole lives underground. With the exception of a few salamander species, all troglobionts are invertebrates; they include gastropods, millipedes, scorpions, harvestmen, and of course, beetles. Beetles are everywhere, aren't they?

We imagine caves as dark, cold, damp, inhospitable places, where food and oxygen are scarce and animals must overcome many dangers and a permanent lack of resources. On the positive side, a deep cave is a place with a constant temperature and humidity, unbothered by the scorching heat of summer or the severe frosts of winter. Some species have adapted for life in never-ending darkness; first and foremost, they have lost their eyes and wings, for which they have no use. They have also lost unnecessary patterns of color and pigment. Most troglofauna are uniformly brown, yellow, or practically translucent. Some have lost the ability to reproduce so that only females live in the caves, reproducing with unfertilized eggs. The pale-yellow blind fly *Troglocladius hajdi*, which lives deep in the Lukina Jama cave in Croatia, is a case in point. Yet this creature has fully developed wings that are capable of flight, making it the only known exception among insect troglobionts in this regard.

Cave insects may have the advantage of a constant temperature, but their sources of food differ from those enjoyed by related species above the surface. They include bat excrement (guano), carrion, and rotting vegetation, which enter their home space via subterranean streams, small soil fauna (e.g., springtails), and of course, the ubiquitous bacteria that feed on cave-insect larvae. Subterranean food sources are so scarce that some adult insects no longer eat at all. All troglobionts conserve energy and move about cave walls very slowly.

Cave beetles include well-known families that live mainly above the surface. Among these are ground beetles (Carabidae) and round fungus beetles (Leiodidae). In many cases, such beetles have short elytra and extraordinarily long legs in relation to the body. Two of these are shown in the picture. The ground beetle *Aphaenopidius treulandi* and the round fungus beetle *Leptodirus hochenwartii* live in the caves of the Dinaric Karst, in the borderlands of Slovenia, Italy, and Croatia. The Leptodirus has a receptor known as the Hamann organ on its antennae, which enables it to perceive air humidity levels.

Not all the world's caves have an endemic, specially adapted troglofauna. In regions whose underground spaces were filled with ice in the Ice Age, all fauna was rendered extinct. This explains why we do not find troglobionts in Europe north of the Alps, or in parts of Asia and North America once covered by glaciers. Because of this, discoveries of unique animals in the cave systems of Central America, China, Southern Europe, and other regions of the world with unexplored underground spaces are all the more valuable. Many surprises still lie in store for us: it is estimated that 90 percent of all caves remain undiscovered!

« *The cave endemites* Leptodirus hochenwartii *(foreground) and* Aphaenopidius treulandi *(background). Both beetles are blind and wingless.*

# FARMER ANTS

*Ants of the genera* Atta *and* Myrmecocystus *(Hymenoptera: Formicidae)*

*The worker of the leaf-cutter ant* Atta cephalotes *has a massive head with powerful mandibles*

Myrmecocystus *honeypot ants hanging from the ceiling of the anthill, their abdomens filled with nutritious fluid*

Large ant colonies are complex "state" organizations comprised of workers, soldiers, a queen and her entourage, nurses, foragers, and many other occupations. Scientists describe such colonies as "superorganisms", as ant individuals work together for the benefit of all, solving complex matters in the process. As they work, they communicate with one another by scent, sound, and touch. Each nest contains only one reproducing queen, who is fertilized by a male during the nuptial flight, when both sexes have wings that enable them to fly. Having found a place suitable for establishing a new colony, a future queen will proceed to lay eggs there, from which infertile workers will be born. Some species colonize by different strategies, including larvae hatched from unfertilized eggs, or marauder and slave-making ants, which we discussed in an earlier chapter. Colonies last for many years. What is more, the queens of certain species are record-holding insects in terms of longevity: they can live for up to 30 years!

Ants have developed several special feeding strategies, some of which we discuss here. Many ant species are predatory, some feed on carrion, others are indirectly herbivorous. The latter method of obtaining food depends on symbiosis with their gut microbes, which allows ants to take nutrients from plant materials. Leafcutter ants (of the genus *Atta*) are widespread in Central and South America. Their huge colonies may be comprised of between 5 and 10 million individuals and reach a depth of 23 feet below the earth. Specialist workers cut up leaves before carrying the pieces into the underground nest. There, other specialist workers cultivate fungus related to the meadow mushroom, the colony's only food. (From the original anthill, the queen who established the colony brings to the new nest a mycelium, which her offspring will cause to reproduce.) There are also specialist workers for fertilizing fungus, weeding, and cultivating antifungal bacteria *Pseudonocardia*, the last for removing unwanted fungi. More special workers deal with the colony's waste. These are excluded from the life of the community, since they may be contaminated with diseases and toxins; they live on piles of waste, and other ants may kill them if they try to return to the nest.

Leaf-cutter ants have much in common with human farmers. The Central American genus *Myrmecocystus*, known as the honeypot ant, has specialist workers used by other workers as living larders for storing sweet juices. The former hang immobile from the ceilings of corridors in the nest; their outstretched abdomens are filled with nutritious "honey" for consumption in an emergency. In territorial battles between colonies of the same honeypot ant species, the victor steals the larvae of the vanquished and transports these live stores to its nest.

There are countless interesting things about the world of ants. The great variety of ant ways of life and their ability to adapt to all kinds of conditions, their combative nature, their teamwork in service of the colony—all these things have made ants extraordinarily successful in evolutionary terms. Myrmecologists estimate that the weight of all ants on Earth is approximately the same as that of all humanity!

« Atta cephalotes *leaf-cutter ants with cut leaves marching along a twig as if along a road, on their way to the anthill.*

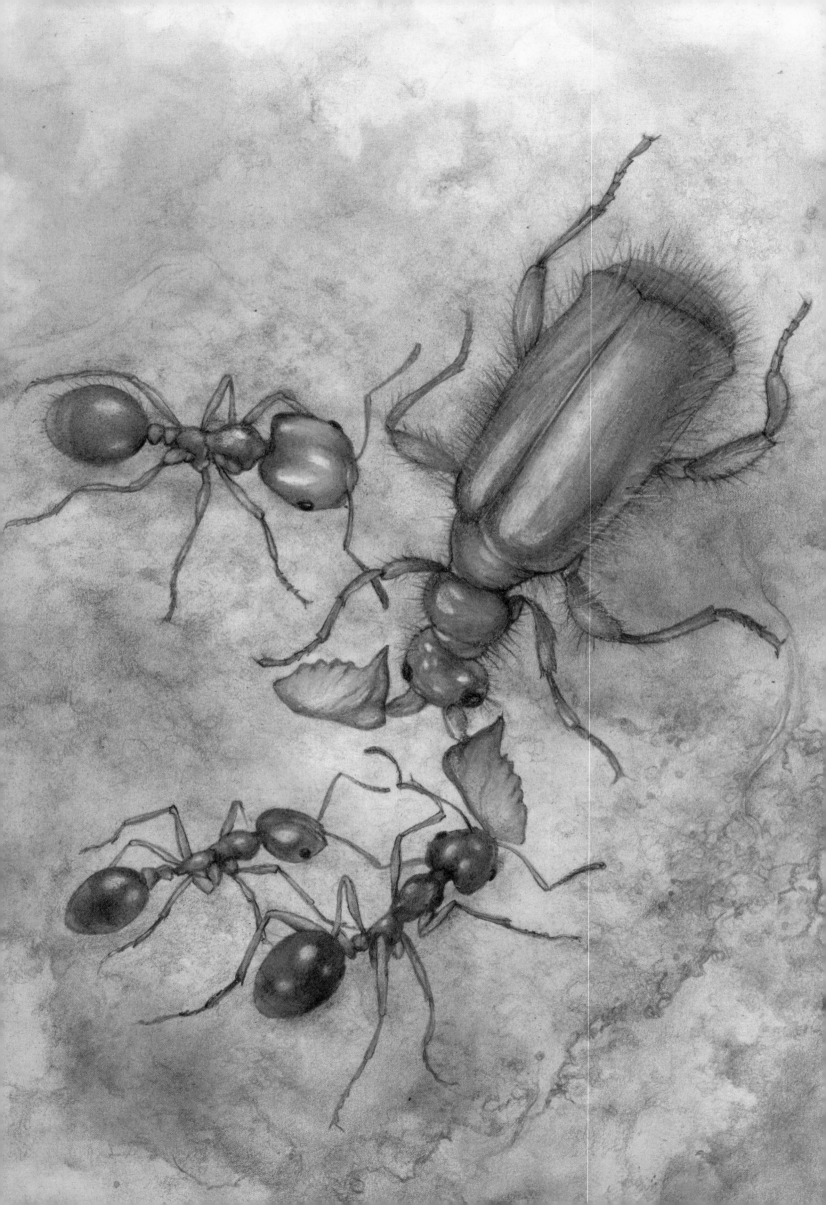

# COEXISTENCE

*Gossamer-winged butterflies (Lycaenidae) and ant nest beetles of the subfamily Paussinae (Carabidae)*

Cerapterus herrei:
*Philippines*

Euplatyhopalus vexillifer:
*India and Bhutan*

Platyrhopalopsis picteti:
*India, Myanmar, and Thailand*

Platyrhopalus paussoides:
*India, Nepal, and Bhutan*

As we have shown, anthills are places of amazing, mysterious happenings, in which the heroes are primarily ants but also other insects. We find myrmecophilous insect species (myrmecophiles spend at least part of their lives in association with ants) among beetles, although there are aphid myrmecophiles and butterfly myrmecophiles too. The latter include gossamer-winged butterflies (Lycaenidae), whose larvae live inside the anthill. In the world as a whole, there are over 6,000 species of gossamer-winged butterflies, making it one of the largest butterfly families; about three quarters of these species are myrmecophiles. Their females lay their eggs on nutritious plants. After hatching, caterpillars nibble at the flowers or leaves of these plants for a while before descending to the ground, where they begin to attract ants. They do so by producing a sweet secretion from glands on their backs. The ants lick at this, then bear the caterpillar away to the anthill. In daytime, ants bring the caterpillars out of the nest so that they may feed on their nutritious plants. Ants return caterpillars to the safety of the nest for the night. Ants and caterpillars communicate by means of sounds and vibrations carried by the firm parts of the anthill. The myrmecophilia of the gossamer-winged butterflies includes mutually beneficial relationships but also parasitic ones; the caterpillar of some butterflies species even eats ant larvae.

Other insects that share their home with ants are the ground beetles of the subfamily Paussinae. We know very little about their larvae, since we mainly find only the adult in an anthill. Paussines are related to small bombardier beetles known as Brachyninae, and like them they have a gland in the abdomen that sprays out a chemical cocktail over 200°F hot that makes an audible explosion, effectively repelling an enemy. They would never use this spray inside a host ant nest, of course. In appearance, paussines are unlike most other ground beetles; they are broad and flat, with thick legs not designed for running and huge, weird-shaped antennae. Unlike gossamer-winged butterflies, paussines don't enrich the lives of the ants they live with; quite the opposite, in fact. The beetles follow the paths made by the ants and can imitate the sound made by the ant queen. By the stridulatory (sound) organs on the elytra, legs and thorax, and substances secreted by the glands in the antennae, they can communicate acoustically and chemically with ants so as not to excite them and thereby cause their expulsion from the nest. In this way, paussines avert the suspicions of worker ants and deceive their hosts. Not only do they live in the safety of the anthill, but they also feed on ant larvae and eggs; some species even pierce ant larvae and soft ant abdomens with their sharp mandibles and suck out their body fluid, known as hemolymph. A relationship between animals by which one benefits and the other does not is called *commensalism* (literally "eating at the same table"). Not only do paussines provide ants with nothing, but they also feed on their immature stages. Even so, there are so few beetles in an anthill that they can do no real harm to the amazing ant superorganism, and so they represent no threat for the colony.

« *In the corridor of an anthill,* Pheidole *workers sniff the antennae of the ant nest beetle* Paussus favieri. *The latter lives from France down to Morocco.*

# THE ART OF DECEPTION

*Brush-footed butterflies (Nymphalidae) and swallowtail butterflies (Papilionidae)*

*Harmless swallowtail butterfly* Papilio polytes *from Southeast Asia*

*Harmless brush-footed butterfly* Hypolimnas misippus *called the Danaid eggfly*

*Inedible Asian swallowtail butterfly* Pachliopa aristolochiae

*Toxic brush-footed butterfly* Danaus chrysippus *called the African queen*

Most insects are small and harmless and lack the strength, teeth, and claws needed for self-defense against insectivorous creatures such as birds, bats, small predatory mammals, and frogs. An insect's most effective weapons in the face of attack are concealment (its ability to blend in with its environment), a warning stance (it pretends to be far larger than it actually is), a toxic sting (in the course of their evolution, some insects have equipped themselves with substances disgusting or even poisonous for others), and reliance on the power of the group. We have discussed some of these vital strategies already. The ones we haven't we will present in the chapters to come.

To confuse enemies, insects do some really amazing things. As examples, we will take several butterfly species who make the most of their coloring. The forests of tropical and subtropical South America are inhabited by zebra longwing (*Heliconius charithonia*) butterflies, which sit on passionflowers to feed on their nectar and pollen grains. From these, they produce toxic substances that make them inedible for predators. Zebra longwings have a bold black-and-yellow-striped wing pattern. To increase their threat, at night they form groups of dozens of individuals. Another peculiarity of this species is that its females are fertilized before they fly from the pupa. Males seek out female pupae by the smell of their pheromones and then watch over them, or else engage in fights with other males until the female in the pupa completes her sexual development. As mating occurs through the pupa, females have no opportunity to participate in sexual selection.

Other South American species of the subfamily Heliconiinae have worked out a rather different self-defense strategy. The postman butterfly (*Heliconius melpomene*) and

the red postman (*H. erato*) sit on poisonous passionflowers and use their pollen grains to produce substances that make them disgusting to predators. The very similar coloration of the two species coevolved to multiply their warning effect on predators, who thus learn to recognize it more easily. This phenomenon is known as Müllerian mimicry. Like the zebra longwing, the postman and the red postman roost in groups of dozens of individuals. Not only are the latter two species very similar, but they also live together. These species do not exchange partners, however; they see differences in the ultraviolet light spectrum and they use pheromones of different chemical composition.

Batesian mimicry is an even more interesting trick used by insects to scare away enemies. Harmless species imitate the body shape and coloration of poisonous or otherwise dangerous species. Once again, we see this in butterflies. The inedible African queen (*Danaus chrysippus*), which is widespread in many places of the world, is imitated by many harmless, unrelated species, one of which is the danaid eggfly (*Hypolimnas misippus*). The harmless Asian swallowtail butterfly (*Papilio polytes*) imitates the inedible common rose (*Pachliopta aristolochiae*). (Both of these pairs are shown in the small illustrations.) Batesian mimics are common among the various orders of insects. Aggressive stinging wasps are the most imitated; among many others, their imitators include harmless hover flies and clearwing moths. This phenomenon, known as aposematism, is the opposite of the camouflaging by which some creatures try to blend in with their environment. Humans, too, use black-and-yellow stripes—to mark places of potential danger, such as steps and railings. Nature has been using such a pattern as a warning for millions of years.

« *A postman butterfly* (Heliconius melpomene) *sitting on a poisonous flower of the passionflower* (Passiflora). *A similarly inedible red postman* (Heliconius erato) *is flying around, with its caterpillar at rest on a leaf. Both butterflies pass the night in groups.*

# MIMICRY AND THE ARMS RACE

*Robber flies (Asilidae), moths and tiger moths (Erebidae),
brush-footed butterflies (Nymphalidae), swallowtail butterflies (Papilionidae)*

*The peacock butterfly* (Inachis io)
*shows off its striking eyespots*

*Garden tiger moth* (Arctiacaja)
*with wings spread and folded*

In this chapter, we will look at some more amazing examples of insects' ability to imitate dangerous creatures and defend themselves against predatory attacks, These will again be cases of Batesian mimicry, but here the defenseless insect imitates not a toxic or stinging insect but a large animal.

In the natural world, evolutionary arms races are constantly in progress. For self-defense, insects take on a deceptive appearance and learn their enemies' strategies. Over generations, predators, on the other hand, have developed ever more new tricks for use in the hunt. The opposite of defensive mimicry is aggressive mimicry, in which the predator attempts to confuse the prey by imitating the prey's behavior. Below, we will look at how predatory blinking fireflies do this. The North American robber fly known as the Florida bee killer (*Mallophora bomboides*), a specialist at hunting bumblebees, is a very interesting case. This fly really does succeed in making itself look like a bumblebee. It does this not to approach the bumblebees unnoticed, however—it doesn't lack for speed—but to scare away its own bird enemies, which also have an eye on the bumblebee. We see now that this is another case of defensive Batesian mimicry.

Evolution often provides small animals with qualities we wouldn't expect them to have. It is well known that bats use echolocation to find their prey. Every night, an acoustic battle is waged between bats and moths, which have developed an ability for defensive acoustic mimicry. Some moths use sound to disrupt bats' ability of echolocation. A tiger moth (*Cycnia tenera*) from South America emits an ultrasound signal to bats, warning them of their inedibility. Other species of completely harmless nocturnal moths of the pyralid family imitate the warning sounds of the *Cycnia tenera* to confuse bats.

Eyespots are a common phenomenon in the natural world. Reef fish have them, as do some snakes. Most of all, insects have them. They serve to frighten enemies and discourage them from attacking an otherwise harmless creature. The European peacock (*Inachis io*), for instance, looks much larger when it opens its wings; a bird attacker suddenly sees a creature much larger than itself staring back from a flower. We find the best-known wearers of eyespots among diurnal butterflies, but mantises and stick insects have them too. To scare away an enemy, it is sometimes enough to briskly open one's boldly colored underwings, as the tiger moth (*Arctia*) and some locusts do.

Adult insects are not the only ones to engage in Batesian mimicry. Adults can at least fly away, but slow, helpless larvae represent a welcome snack for a bird. But imagine the bird's surprise when it finds a snake looming over it! The caterpillar of the African swallowtail *Papilio demodocus* feeds on citrus leaves. On the edges of the front of its body it has dark spots that look like eyes, and when seen from the front or above, it looks much larger and wider than it actually is. In addition, it has an *osmeterium*—a "two-horned," orange-colored growth behind the head that looks like a snake's tongue. All swallowtail caterpillars have this. When disturbed, they thrust it out to emit a foul-smelling substance.

Though apparently defenseless, insects deploy several tricks to ensure their survival. The simplest of these strategies is strength in numbers, as the mayfly has shown us. Different forms of mimicry, like the imitation of dangerous creatures, are far more complex. So, too, is the ability to hide well, as we shall see in the next chapter.

« *The caterpillar of* Papilio demodocus *feeds on citrus leaves. Its head resembles that of a snake with a forked tongue. Above the caterpillars here we see a swallowtail in flight. It has hatched from the pupa in the background.*

# GIANT INSECTS AND THE ART OF CONCEALMENT

## Spectra (Phasmatodea)

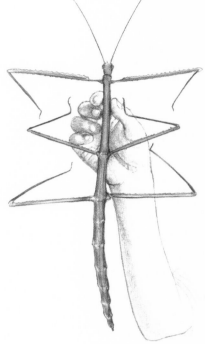

*Australian spiny leaf insect*
(Extatosoma tiaratum)

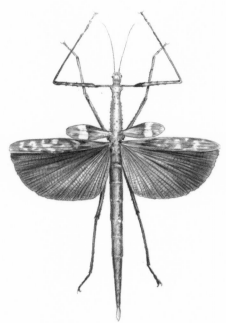

*The stick insect* Phobaeticus chani,
*the world's longest insect*

*Unlike other stick insects, the Australian*
Acrophylla wuelfingi *has fully developed
wings and warning coloration*

The romantic notion of tropical forests filled with enormous beetles and ants, great stinging wasps, and huge colorful butterflies is misleading. The vast majority of the million-plus known insect species are but a few millimeters long. The biomass (total volume) of tropical and subtropical insects is for the most part composed of ants, termites, small leafhoppers, and beetles that are not much larger or more colorful than their relatives in temperate climes. Even so, the biodiversity of insects in the tropics is amazing; among many less conspicuous species we find creatures remarkable in shape and striking in color. The great variety of nutritious plants and food options in the tropics has given rise to a huge number of forms of insect life, among whom there is an ongoing battle for resources, including "arms races" between predator and prey. In the favorable conditions of tropical and subtropical forests, many giant insect species have emerged out of the constant pressures of natural selection.

Which is the biggest? In terms of body length, the answer to this is clear: the tropical spectra (Phasmatodea) order of stick insects. Certain species of this remarkable insect are over a foot long! For many years it was thought that the insect with the longest body (about one foot long) was the stick insect *Phryganistria fruhstorferi*, which was described in 1907 as being present in China and Burma (modern-day Myanmar). It was superseded by the similar *Phobaeticus kirbyi* stick insect from Borneo, of which there is a museum specimen measuring just over one foot long. Since 2008, the "king" of the giant insects has been a relative of the Bornean species known as Chan's megastick

(*Phobaeticus chani*); its body length alone is 1.2 feet long, and with legs outstretched it measures an unbelievable 1.8 feet long!

All spectra are masters of camouflage. Some are slender with long legs resembling twigs. We call these stick insects. Brownish-gray in color, they are not very mobile; some have wings but many are wingless. When in scrub or on the stems of larger herbs, they are difficult to see, not least as they sway to mimic the movement of a plant in a breeze. Other spectra species are more robust, with spined bodies and extensible legs that allow them to blend in with spined scrub and leaves. The final body type is that of the leaf insects (*Phylliidae*), which have a flat body and extensible legs and are mostly green—often making them indistinguishable from real leaves. Spectra can defend themselves with the spined femurs of the hind legs or by a stinking secretion. They can also intimidate an enemy by spreading their brightly colored wings.

In other ways, spectra are unremarkable insects. They move through vegetation slowly and spend their lives grazing on green leaves. Smaller species are often found in insectaria, as they are easy to care for; they can be fed leaves of blackberry or ivy all year round. It is easy, too, for spectra kept as pets to reproduce. As females of many species lay unfertilized eggs, no male is needed for reproduction; in the wild, males tend to be a rarity. Spectra undergo incomplete metamorphosis. Immediately after hatching, nymphs resemble adults (or mimic larger ants), and they have the same plant-food diet.

« *The huge but defenseless wingless stick insect* Phryganistria fruhstorferi *sitting motionless, mimicking a twig.*

# A POOL IN A STREAM

*Rove beetles (Staphylinidae), whirligig beetles (Gyrinidae), and riffle beetles (Elmidae)*

*The eyes of all whirligig beetles are divided into a higher and a lower pair*

*Thanks to a secretion from glands on its abdomen, the rove beetle* Stenus guttula *can change the surface tension of water, run on the surface, or dive in*

*The aquatic larva of the whirligig beetle is predatory*

Clean flowing waters and their banks abound with insect life. Beetles live in crystal-clear pools in woodland streams just as they live in raging waterfalls, which goes to show that insects can adapt to extreme conditions. As we have seen with mayflies and dragonflies, some evolutionarily primitive insect groups with incomplete metamorphosis have aquatic larvae known as nymphs—a form of life we know to have existed since the Carboniferous Period of the Palaeozoic Era, over 300 million years ago. For this reason, it is possible that the life cycle of prehistoric "insects" bound them to fresh water. Most of today's insects are permanently terrestrial; in the course of their evolution, they lost the ability to breathe underwater. Some evolutionarily advanced groups returned to an aquatic environment; the terrestrial predecessors of whales (in the Tertiary Period) are a case in point.

Beetles are the most numerous animal group on Earth, so it will come as no surprise that we find the greatest number of returnees to the water among beetles. It is simplest to adapt to life on sandbanks or mudbanks next to water; it is here that small ground beetles (Carabidae), rove beetles (Staphylinidae), and variegated mud-loving beetles (Heteroceridae) run about and build shelters. Some of them have special adaptations. *Paederus* rove beetles, for instance, have striking, aposematic coloration, by which they give warning of vesicant toxins in their body fluid. Their abundance on the banks of the Nile River in Egypt has led some scientists to believe them to be the originator of one of the Ten Plagues of Egypt, as described in the Bible. Rove beetles of the genus *Stenus* can run on water, and also to go underwater in case of need.

Beetles living in wet moss under waterfalls in swift-flowing streams have a strange way of life. Members of the longtoed water beetle (Dryopidae) and riffle beetle (Elmidae) families, they stay in swift-flowing water thanks to the large claws on their feet. Although adults cannot swim, they spend most of their life in water, attached to wet rocks, feeding on algae and small organisms (e.g., biofilms), and breathing bubbles of air attached to the thick hairs of their body. Their larvae often live in water too.

Perhaps the most amazing adaptation to the environment of the freshwater pond is demonstrated by whirligig beetles (Gyrinidae). Active hunters, they use their natatory (meaning "swimming"), fringed legs to move in rapid circles on the surface. They remain in swarms as a form of self-defense; when in danger, they are agile divers. Underwater, they breathe bubbles of air attached to the intricate arrangement of hair on their abdomen. Whirligig beetles are also excellent flyers capable of settling in a new place, such as a garden swimming pool; when conditions become unfavorable, they will fly away. They have divided eyes. When they swim on the surface, one pair of eyes looks up at the sky, while the other, submerged pair looks into the water. Whirligig beetle larvae live in the water and are predatory. They develop from eggs laid by the female on stems of aquatic plants, to which she is attached by her long front legs. Despite these extraordinary adaptations, whirligig beetles have been around for a very long time. Fossil finds testify to their existence 200 million years ago, in the Lower Jurassic Period, as well as that of very similar beetles over 250 million years ago, in the Permian Period.

« *Poisonous* Paederus *rove beetles live on the shores of streams. Here, the dark-colored riffle beetle* (Stenelmis canaliculata) *is catching stones. A group of quick-diving whirligig beetles are swimming in a shallow pool.*

# UNDERWATER DANGER

*Giant water bugs (Belostomatidae) and water boatmen (Notonectidae)*

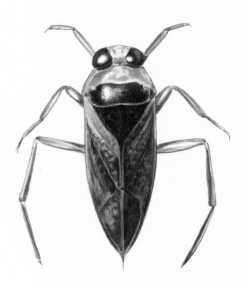

*Common backswimmer* (Notonecta glauca)

*Male of the genus* Belostoma, *with eggs stuck to his back*

The murky waters of the paddy fields of Southeast Asia represent a lethal danger to small fish and amphibians. This is the home of giant predatory true bugs of the genus *Lethocerus*, which sometimes go for prey larger than they are. Labyrinth fish, colorful creatures adapted for life in the waters of low oxygenation of rice fields and temporary monsoon pools, are especially vulnerable to attack. These fish, which include well-known "aquarium" paradise fish, gouramies, and Siamese fighting fish, replenish their oxygen supply by breathing air on the surface. As they do so, they may fall victim to attacks from true bugs lurking in aquatic plants. The bugs grip the fish between the spines of their upper and lower front legs before applying a venomous stylet.

All true bugs have piercing-sucking mouthparts called stylets, which are folded under the head when at rest. Predatory species use their stylet to inject the prey with clotting proteins and digestive enzymes that break down tissue. They then suck out the victim.

Over twenty species of the genus *Lethocerus* are spread across warm regions of all continents, including Southern Europe. The largest such species is up to 5 inches long; despite its size, it is an excellent flyer that moves from one body of water to the next. Its sting is very painful for humans, yet in Asia it is hunted (mainly at night, by attraction to light) and appears at farmers markets (local people cook it in oil).

Including *Lethocerus*, Belostomatidae consists of almost 200 predatory true bug species. Some of these are remarkable for the care they take of their offspring. *Lethocerus* males guard eggs laid on aquatic plants. As for species of other genera, notably the American *Belostoma* and *Abedus*, the female finds a male with whom to mate before laying her eggs on the male's back, where the male will carry them until they hatch.

While Belostomatidae giant water bugs swim underwater, coming to the surface in the usual way, their smaller relatives the water boatmen (Notonectidae) are remarkable in that they swim on the surface upside down. Thanks to its long, hair-fringed hind legs, the water boatman is a much better swimmer than the giant water bug. Along with its inverted swimming style, it developed inverted coloration: its "back" is light while its "belly" is dark. As a result, when viewed from above it blends in with the bottom of the body of water, and when viewed from below it merges with the sky. Though only about 1 cm in length, water boatmen are predatory and have a keen sting; for the latter reason, they are sometimes referred to as "water bees". Another family of water boatmen, Corixidae, swims in the usual way and in most cases is herbivorous rather than carnivorous. Some Corixidae species live in salt water, making them a rare exception among insects.

« *Giant true bug* (Lethocerus) *catching a paradise fish* (Macropodus opercularis).

# CARRIERS OF DISEASE

*Kissing bugs (Reduviidae) and tsetse flies (Glossinidae)*

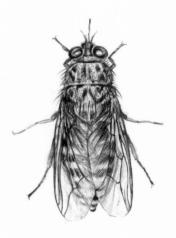

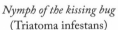

*Nymph of the kissing bug*
(Triatoma infestans)

*Adult kissing bug*
(Triatoma infestans)

*Tsetse fly*
(Glossina morsitans)

Although insect life includes many interesting, useful creatures on which the lives of many plants and animals depend, some insects bring great danger. A significant number are vectors of harmful diseases. The mosquitoes are a well-known case in point, as carriers of malaria or the Zika virus, as are fleas as spreaders of plague.

In tropical America and Africa, parasitic protozoa known as trypanosomes represent a great threat. America's *Trypanosoma cruzi* attacks many wild and domestic animals, including humans, in whom it causes a long-drawn-out condition known as Chagas disease. Carriers of these trypanosomes include the kissing or vampire bugs of the subfamily *Triatominae* (of the family Reduviidae), which are at home primarily in tropical and subtropical America. Our picture shows the species *Triatoma dimidiata*, which lives across Mexico and Peru. Its way of life is shared by many other vampire bugs. *Triatoma dimidiata* is a relatively large true bug; adults are 2–3 cm long and characterized by a large, tough stylet that is curled under the body when at rest. In daytime, kissing bugs congregate in large groups on tree trunks and palms; at night, they seek out warm-blooded animals such as birds in nests, rodents, bats, and marsupials, whose blood they suck through their stylet. Unlike malaria-spreading mosquitoes, kissing bugs do not transmit trypanosomes by sucking. Protozoa develop in a kissing bug's digestive tract and come out in its feces. Should these come into contact with a wound on a host's body, they will soon reside in the host's organs, such as the heart, liver, or brain. From there, they will gradually be released into the blood, from which they may again be sucked by a kissing bug, thereby closing the development cycle of trypanosomes. Chagas disease can also be transmitted between hosts directly through the blood; in humans, it is a serious, protracted illness with no known reliable cure. It is often said that Chagas disease was the cause of the long-term health problems of Charles Darwin, who caught it as a young man in South America on the HMS *Beagle* during a research expedition.

Other harmful trypanosomes transmitted by insects include three subspecies of *Trypanosoma brucei* and at least four other trypanosome species from tropical Africa. These parasitic protozoa cause a sleeping sickness that is a menace in rural areas. Unlike Chagas disease, it is transmitted not by true bugs but by tsetse flies (*Glossina*). In tropical Africa, there are over 20 tsetse species. As well as causing disease in humans, they transmit it to cattle too. In cattle, this sickness is known as nagana or surra. The tsetse transmits protozoa through its stylet, sucking blood in the full glare of the daytime sun. Reproduction of trypanosomes takes place in the fly's body; after complex development, the infectious parasite reaches the fly's salivary glands, from where it can be transmitted through the stylet to mammals including humans. Although humans and cattle who contract this disease suffer greatly, and often die if no treatment is found, animals in the wild manage the infection much better. The tsetse is sometimes referred to as the "protector of the wild": in the past, areas infested with the sleeping sickness were unsuitable for human colonization and the conversion of the African wilderness into fields and pasture lands.

« Triatoma dimidiata *kissing bugs keep to a tree trunk in the day before moving to a birds' nest in the evening.*

# LETHAL BEAUTY

## *Mantises (Mantodea)*

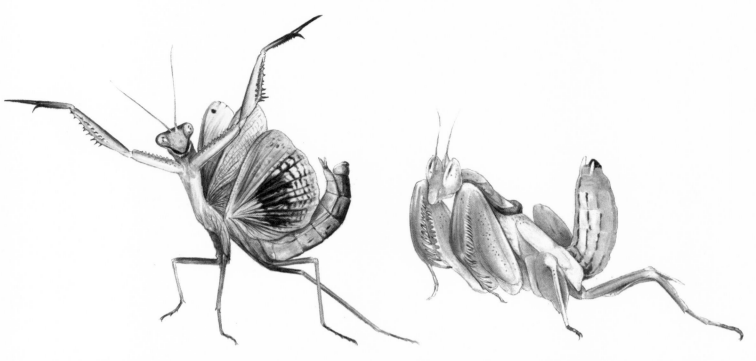

*Mediterranean mantis* (Iris oratoria) *in a threatening stance*

*The walking flower mantis* (Hymenopus coronatus) *from tropical Asia camouflages itself as an orchid flower*

Raptorial front legs equipped with sharp spines evolved independently in several groups of arthropods, including the mantis shrimp. Such legs occur in several unrelated insect orders, including predatory aquatic true bugs and mantid lacewings. In some herbivorous stick insects, the spined hind legs serve for protection. The mantises have developed raptorial legs to a state of perfection. Sharp spines of different lengths on the femur of forelegs run against similarly sharp spines on the tibia, which end in a mighty, curved spike capable of piercing the cuticle of an insect or the skin of a small vertebrate. To trap its prey, the mantis holds the victim between the spines of the femur and the tibia of forelegs; if need be, it pierces the prey with the spike at the end of the tibia. As if all this were not enough, the front coxae of a mantis have tooth-like spurs. Thus the forelegs as a whole form a deadly weapon that allows the mantises to hunt prey larger than itself. It intimidates enemies by waving and raising the forelegs.

Mantises have many other interesting adaptations. The head of a mantis is relatively small, triangular, and extraordinarily mobile; it can be rotated up to 180°. As its two bulbous eyes point to the sides, we believe it to be one of the few insects with stereo vision. In addition, mantises have three simple eyes on the forehead that perceive light, a remnant of their primitive insect ancestors. Mantises are related to cockroaches, survivors from the Carboniferous Period, although the oldest fossils of mantises hitherto discovered are from the early Cretaceous Period, making them 145 million years old.

Mantises are masters of camouflage. They can disguise themselves as a plant stalk, a herb leaf, even a colorful flower. A mantis blends in with vegetation as it lies in wait for prey, which it snaps up with a quick lunge of the forelegs. Most of its prey is insect life, although sometimes it attacks an animal much larger than itself, such as a lizard or a gecko. Such an attack does not always end well for the mantis; the predator may well become the prey. Even so, we know of cases of a mantis disguised as a flower mounting a successful attack on a hummingbird that has come for its nectar.

How mantises reproduce is an interesting topic too. Far smaller than the female, the male must be on guard in the mating season. Although the female may consent to fertilization by him, this does not mean that the male is safe. Her flexible, mobile head makes it possible for her to turn on the male during copulation, when she may choose to eat him. This phenomenon is known as sexual cannibalism. Even so, the male can continue the copulation act with his head bitten off! Males of some species try to avoid such a fate by presenting the female with an insect catch, in the hope that she will feed on this nuptial gift until the act of copulation is complete.

Mantis eggs, like those of the cockroaches, are laid in a hard capsule (known as an ootheca) attached to a vegetation stalk. In common with those of some stick insects, its nymphs often mimic the body shape of an ant. In cold regions, the ootheca hibernates; the small mantises hatch together in spring and reach adulthood in summer. As a rule, the female lives longer than the male, surviving until the autumn.

« *European mantis* (Mantis religiosa) *catching a lizard.*

# SABER-TOOTHED HUNTERS
*Tiger beetles (Coleoptera: Carabidae: Cicindelinae)*

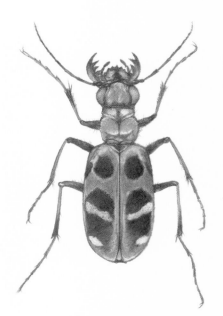

*Japanese tiger beetle*
(Cicindela chinensis japonica)

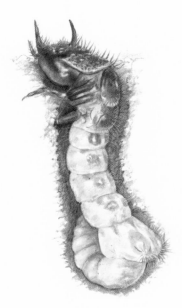

Manticora *tiger beetle larva*
*in its burrow*

Cicindela campestris,
*a widespread Eurasian tiger beetle*

Many insect species or groups have come to symbolize certain human characteristics or cultural phenomena. Butterflies represent inconstancy, while flies and mosquitoes are associated with meddling. The mantis is a symbol of the femme fatale, a dangerous yet alluring woman. In the naming of new animal genera and species, the scientists who discover and describe them are often inspired by culture, not least literature and mythology. The works of J. R. R. Tolkien, for instance, are as rich in entomological terminology as they are in reference to ancient myths. In 1781, a genus of the tiger beetles of the ground beetle family (Carabidae: Cicindelinae) was given the name "Manticora", after celebrated zoologist Johan Christian Fabricius was inspired by the mantichore, a figure in Persian mythology that takes the form of a man-eating lion with the face of a human and a tail of venomous spines. This monster was taken up by Greek mythology. In the European Middle Ages, it appeared in illustrated bestiaries and on coats of arms; it is even mentioned in poetry.

The Manticora tiger beetle, too, can be considered a monstrous killer. All species are dark brown, large, and bulky, and up to 2 inches long. The head is dominated by huge, scythe-like mandibles, which are asymmetrical in the male. The manticoras are nocturnal predators that avoid the midday heat by staying in a burrow. They live in southern Africa, for the most part in the deserts and semi-deserts of Angola and Mozambique and right down to the tip of South Africa. They use their mandibles in the hunt for insects, typically crickets and locusts. We can't be sure why

the mandibles are so strikingly asymmetrical; the male sometimes uses them to grip the female during copulation.

As hunters, manticora larvae are no less ruthless than the adult beetle, but their strategy is very different: while beetles can run quickly on long, slender legs, a larva's body is buried in the ground perpendicular, with only the carapaced pronotum and the sharp mandibles exposed. The carapace closes off the burrow like a lid. As the prey approaches, the larva flies out of the ground at an incredible speed and grabs the prey in its mandibles before pulling it into its burrow. In this lightning attack, sometimes only the head, sometimes more of the body emerges.

In African folklore, the manticora is shown as a creature of the devil because of its appearance and nocturnal and predatory nature; sometimes it is a personification of Death. It appears in several places in European literature, from Dante to Jules Verne. In Verne's novel *Dick Sand, A Captain at Fifteen*, the character Cousin Benedict chases a flying manticora. The manticoras have stunted wings, and none of their 5 to 10 species can fly. As for tiger beetles in general, they are found all over the world, and most of them are excellent flyers. They are found most often on coastal sand dunes, dirt roads, and dry forests, where they hunt ants and other insects. Their larvae, too, look similar and behave in a similar way, although adult tiger beetles and larvae are far smaller than their manticora counterparts. They make up for their small size, however, with their beautiful coloration; the adults sport splendid metallic and pastel shades, from emerald green to flame red.

« *A manticora with a cricket prey in its mandibles. In the foreground is a manticora larva in its burrow, with only the head visible.*

# DECEIVED SUITORS
# AND THE BRIGHT BEAUTY OF COLOR
*Jewel beetles (Coleoptera: Buprestidae)*

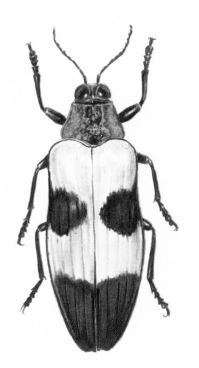

Chrysochroa buqueti,
*from tropical Asia*

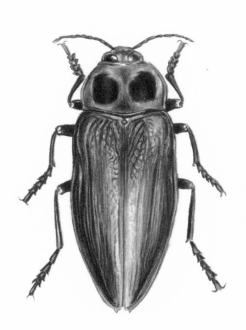

*People of Amazonia make necklaces from the
elytra of the jewel beetle* (Euchroma gigantea)

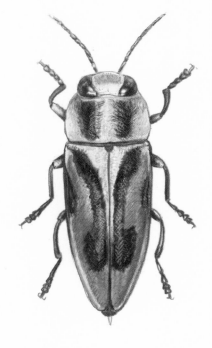

Anthaxia candens,
*the "cherry" jewel beetle*

Jewel beetles (Buprestidae) are a family of beetles with over 15,000 species. Their bodies are characterized by a delightful coloration and shine, a metallic gleam, and muted pastel shades. They include creatures only a few millimeters in length whose larvae "mine", i.e., they live in a hollow between the upper and lower side of a leaf and feed on plant tissue without damaging the skin of the leaf, but also larger species over 3 inches long. Most jewel beetle larvae live in wood or the phloem (plant vascular tissue that takes foods made in the leaves during photosynthesis to all other parts of the plant) of trees or shrubs; adult beetles often rest on flowers. A jewel beetle's striking coloration may be the result of pigment in the cuticle, although a metallic gleam on the elytron (the anterior wing that protects the posterior, functional wing) is caused by texture in the cuticle that reflects light at certain wavelengths, a phenomenon known as structural coloration. Thanks to this, many East Asian and South American cultures traditionally use jewel beetle elytra in jewelry and other decorations.

Jewel beetles are excellent flyers. Like many diurnal insects, they use their large compound eyes to look for partners to mate with. Like bees and diurnal butterflies, however, jewel beetles do not perceive light as humans do. So it happens that large Australian jewel beetles, called *Julodimorpha bakewelli*, can mistake gleaming, discarded beer bottles for females of their own species and attempt copulation with them. What's more, these poor males take the raised indentation and inscription on the base and neck of the bottles for the wrinkled texture of the females' bodies. In the bush, bottles discarded at the roadside are mobbed by male beetles, who spend several hours trying to fertilize them until they die of exhaustion. The fact that the bottles are larger than the female beetle makes them all the more irresistible to the male, an example of supernormal stimulus. Indeed, thanks to the bottles, it may happen that female beetles are left hanging. Discarded beer bottles are a real threat to the lives of beetles—even to the whole species. Their evolution has not prepared the beetles for such a complication, and this change has come too quickly for them to adapt.

In a similar deceit, polarized light attracts insects to the great shiny surfaces of solar panels and, to a lesser extent, the smooth surfaces of garden ponds and swimming pools. Loss of insects is caused not only by the all-night illumination of cities, large-scale deforestation, the chemicalization of agriculture, water pollution, and other obvious suspects; it occurs, too, because of random, unexpected events like the discarding of beer bottles at the roadside. Such things can disrupt the natural balance and lead to the extinction of a species that lived for hundreds of thousands, even millions, of years before people arrived.

« *Males of the jewel beetle* (Julodimorpha bakewelli) *trying to copulate with a beer bottle discarded by a passing truck driver.*

# CARING PARENTS

## Scarab beetles (Scarabaeidae) and bess beetles (Passalidae)

*Cocoon of* Copris hispanus *horned dung beetle (cross-section)*

*Sacred scarab* (Scarabaeus sacer) *rolling a dung ball*

*Burrow of a dung beetle of the genus* Copris *(cross-section)*

Eusocial insects are not the only ones who take good care of their offspring. It is well known that other insect groups with incomplete metamorphosis, such as true bugs and earwigs, protect their eggs and small nymphs. Insects with complete metamorphosis, too, take care of their eggs and larvae. However, perhaps the best known care for offspring is performed by the scarab beetles (Scarabaeidae), one species of which, the sacred scarab (*Scarabaeus sacer*), is often depicted by Ancient Egyptian artists as Khepri, a symbol of the rising sun and rebirth.

Most members of this family process animal droppings for use as food for their larvae. In this regard, let us consider the genus *Copris*, whose care for its larvae is well documented. The horned dung beetle (*C. lunaris*) is widespread across Western Europe and China; it has also been introduced in Australia as an experimental measure for eradicating the droppings of non-native ungulates. Adult dung beetles spend the whole of the warm season on lawns and pastures, using their excellent sense of smell on their comb-like antennae to seek out piles of droppings from domestic cattle. Beneath the dung, they dig a vertical corridor about 6 to 7 inches long. Each corridor ends in a chamber, to which a pair of parent beetles transports between 6 and 8 carefully rolled balls of dung. In the chamber, the balls undergo fermentation, following which the female forms them into a pear shape and lays a single egg in the narrowed end. The beetle couple remains underground, guarding the entrances to their vertical burrows. The female remains with the young throughout their development, meanwhile repairing damaged chambers and guarding burrows and

"cans" of food. Hatched larvae feed on a fermented ball before pupating in a solid spherical cocoon made of dung and soil. After the freshly hatched beetles break through their cocoon, the newborns and their parents (sometimes the male, too, has remained underground) leave the chamber and emerge above ground. The subject of our picture, the *C. hispanus* dung beetle from the Mediterranean, cares for its offspring in a similar way; the male is distinguished from the female by the long horns on his head.

By cleaning up the droppings of large herbivores, the many species of dung beetle play an important role in the natural world. Some species dig vertical corridors up to three feet deep. Some of them (so-called kleptoparasites) steal the food balls of others and lay their eggs in them. Not all dung beetles make vertical burrows; small species in particular make chambers under piles of dung or even in them. It is interesting to note that the African *Scarabaeus satyrus* navigates by the Milky Way during its nighttime operations, the only invertebrate known to do so.

To end, let us mention another group that takes excellent care of its offspring. This is the bess beetles (Passalidae), a small tropical relative to the dung beetles that has a cylindrical body and dark coloration. Bess beetles live in groups in rotting wood. Here they build their corridor systems, and here the females lay their eggs. Adults help larvae prepare their food and make their cocoons. Larvae eat the feces of adults in a kind of external digestion of hard-to-decompose food. Bess beetles—adults and larvae—use up to 14 sound signals. Who would guess that these unremarkable-looking beetles were so sophisticated?

« *An* Ontophagus taurus *male rolling a ball. On the pile of cow dung behind him is a pair of* Copris hispanus *dung beetles and a small* Acrossus luridus.

# BEE HUNTERS

## Asian hornets and Asian giant hornets (Hymenoptera: Vespidae)

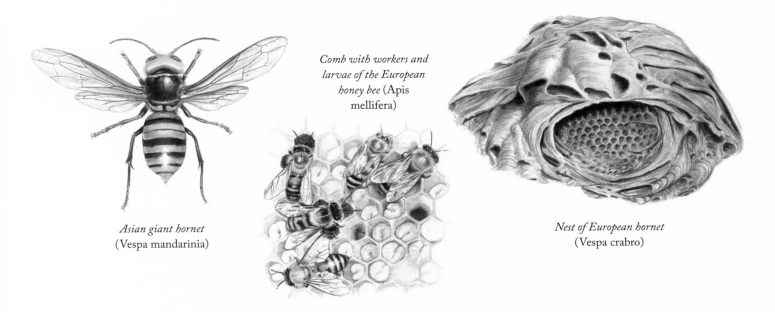

Asian giant hornet
(Vespa mandarinia)

Comb with workers and
larvae of the European
honey bee (Apis
mellifera)

Nest of European hornet
(Vespa crabro)

The species of animals and plants we know today have adapted to changing conditions over millions of years. Insect species have evolved along with their predators, parasites, and prey, and alongside the plants they pollinate or feed on. For many generations, they have competed in a race called coevolution. For this reason, events in the natural world are in a state of constant, dynamic balance. Only rarely does one species render another extinct. This may happen, for example, if a predator for which local wildlife is unprepared arrives on an isolated island or if declining sea level results in the connection of a mainland to a new territory, thereby allowing large beasts of prey to cross, or, if a deadly virus spreads to a local population.

In the current, Anthropocene Epoch (i.e., the era of man), accidental introduction or intentional planting of nonnative species is far more frequent than at other times in history. Nonnative species that spread spontaneously on a new territory are known as invasive species. In many cases, they have a detrimental effect on wildlife and may displace native species.

Whether relocated by humans inadvertently or with good intentions, many small insects have come to be regarded as intruders. Good cases in point are the stinging fire ant *Solenopsis invicta* from South America, the Asian ladybeetle *Harmonia axyridis*, and two aggressive species of East Asian hornets that have conquered the world in recent years.

The Asian giant hornet (*Vespa mandarinia*) is a relative newcomer in the US and Canada. Its worker is over 1 inch long, the queen over 2 inches. Its sting contains a venom comparable to that of the bee, but as there is more venom in the sting and this hornet is aggressive (unlike *V. crabro*, the non-aggressive, barely venomous European hornet), it

is dangerous for humans. Asian giant hornets feed on sweet fruit juices and sap, although they also hunt other insects, not least beetles and caterpillars. At summer's end, they attack the nests of other social insect species, especially wasps and bees; sometimes they attack a nest of their own species. Their targets are unhatched larvae in combs, which they carry away as food for their own larvae. They attack en masse and can destroy an entire colony, which often includes tens of thousands of workers. European honey bees have no effective protection against them and cannot even kill hornet scouts. Eastern honey bees (*Apis cerana*) have greater experience of hornets and patrol their nests. On encountering hornet scouts, they release a pheromone that attracts their own kind. These surround the hornet and literally heat it to death; bees tolerate higher temperatures and levels of carbon dioxide than hornets. If a scout escapes, the bees cover its scent mark with scattered plant scents.

Another invasive hornet species entered France by chance in 2004 and has since spread across Europe. The Asian hornet (*Vespa velutina*) may be smaller than the Asian giant hornet, but it is a very aggressive creature that specializes in bee-hunting. While the adult feeds mostly on sweet juices, it hunts insects, especially bees, for their larvae. For the hives of European honey bees—which lack the defenses of their adapted Asian counterparts—the arrival of Asian hornets means disaster. The hornets patrol the edge of the hive, where they kill worker bees returning home with a load of pollen. With its mandibles, the hornet removes the bee's head and abdomen before taking the nutritious thorax to its larvae in the nest. At summer's end, Asian hornets attack beehives en masse. Unlike giant Asian hornets, however, they do not kill workers on the spot before seizing their combs. Instead, they bear whole slaughtered bees away to their nest.

« *An Asian hornet* (Vespa velutina) *attacking a beehive. The bees are trying in vain to defend the entrance.*

# STRANGE SHAPES

## *Treehoppers (Hemiptera: Membracidae)*

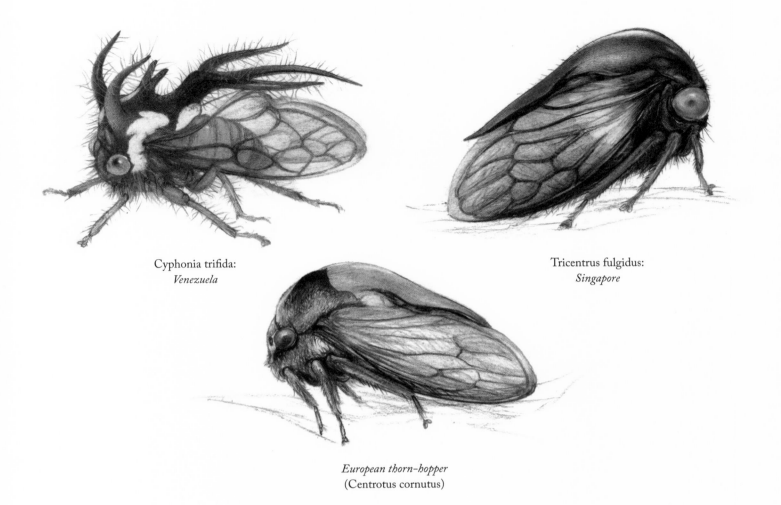

Cyphonia trifida:
*Venezuela*

Tricentrus fulgidus:
*Singapore*

*European thorn-hopper*
(Centrotus cornutus)

Beauty of coloration and remarkable behavior: just two things that make insects so amazing. Although insects are very small, if we observe them through a microscope, or even an ordinary magnifying glass, we get a view of fascinating, highly complex bodily structures. Some small flies and beetles have an enlarged head, with the eyes set on the side, like those of a hammerhead shark. Gleaming scales on butterfly wings, wings transformed into feathers on featherwing beetles (*Ptiliidae*), the intricately shaped antennae of nocturnal moths, the pincers of earwigs—all these things have their purpose, which shows how these insects have adapted to their way of life and environment. But how do we explain the bizarre structures on the body of small jumping creatures related to the cicadas? What on earth can the branching antenna over its whole body length be for? Why does a half-centimeter-long creature have five violet-colored balls on the ends of thorns twice the height of its body?

The creatures in question are thorn bugs (Membracidae), small relatives of cicadas and leafhoppers, with whom they belong to the order Hemiptera (along with aphids, true bugs, and many other small insect groups). Like many of their relatives, thorn bugs impale plant tissue and draw on sap; some species, not least at the nymphal stage, produce a sweet honeydew. As a result, they enter into mutually beneficial relationships with other insects, e.g., ants and wasps, which lick the honeydew and in return provide protection. In one well-known case, gregarious thorn bugs live in a mutualistic relationship with geckos, communicating with them by vibrations in the abdomen. In common with the cicadas, thorn bug males and females communicate by sound, which is at a very high frequency and thus inaudible to the human ear.

The thorn bugs' most remarkable spikes are on the pronotum, the dorsal side of the prothorax. In some cases, this evidently serves as camouflage, by mimicking the thorns and small leaves of the plants it feeds on. Sometimes, however, such a simple explanation does not suffice. The pronotum of many species features fantastical figures reminding us, among other things, of forked thorns, horns, flags, antennae, horseshoes, and twigs; its swellings may be spherical or wrinkled. These intricate figures are hollow, and, as far as we know, do not differ between the sexes. The pictures here show only a small fraction of the great diversity present in over 3,000 thorn bug and treehopper species.

« *Treehoppers from the Brazilian rainforests:* Bocydium globulare *(center)*, Sphongophorus ballista *(top right)*, Umbonia spinosa *(top left)*.

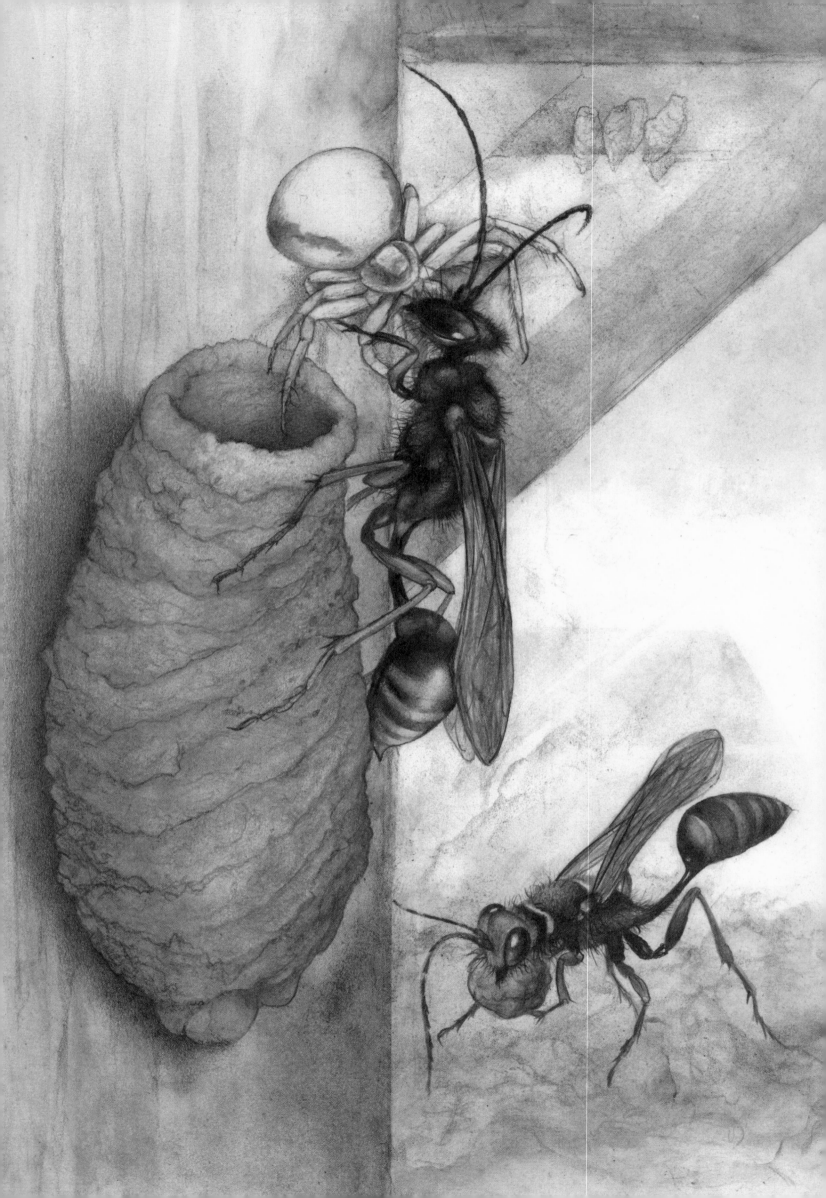

# THE COMPLICATED LIVES OF PARASITES

## Ichneumonids (Ichneumonidae), sand wasps, and mud daubers (Sphecidae)

*Red-banded sand wasp* (Ammophila sabulosa) *with caterpillar catch*

*The female saber wasp* (Rhyssa persuasoria) *drills her ovipositor into a tree trunk*

It has been estimated that parasites account for 80 percent of all biological species. So it should come as no surprise that a parasitic way of life is very common among insects. Ectoparasites live on the outer surface of the host, or even beyond it. They include fleas, lice, mosquitoes, and flies. We find most parasites among Hymenoptera, whose larvae develop inside the bodies of insects of other species, such as butterfly caterpillars. Parasitism inside the host is known as endoparasitism. To make matters more complicated still, many hymenopteran parasites (e.g., ichneumonid wasps) have parasites of their own among the tiny wasps known as chalcids. This phenomenon is known as hyperparasitism. Among hymenopterans, there are even known cases of hyperparasites with their own parasitoid. A parasitoid is a parasite that kills its host.

As an effective measure against herbivorous insect overpopulation, endoparasites are humankind's allies in agriculture and forestry. One such ally is the saber wasp (*Rhyssa persuasoria*), whose female drills her long firm ovipositor up to 1.5 inches into a trunk, where her excellent sense of smell will lead her to horntail (or large longhorn beetle) larvae, into which she will lay her egg through the wood. Hatched saber wasp larvae develop inside the horntail, literally eating it alive. After pupation, the adult saber wasp flies out of the trunk.

The red-banded sand wasp (*Ammophila sabulosa*) is a distant relative of the wasp, and like the wasp it has a venomous sting. It lives a solitary life, however, feeding on nectar from flowers. A fertilized sand wasp female digs a corridor in the ground, then flies about looking for a caterpillar. This caterpillar is often bigger than she is. With her sting, she immobilizes but does not kill it. Then she pulls the defenseless creature into her burrow, where she lays her egg on it. Upon hatching, the sand wasp larva eats the paralyzed caterpillar live before pupating in the burrow. After metamorphosis into an adult, it flies out of the ground.

In recent decades, the Asian mud-dauber wasp (*Sceliphron curvatum*), which is native to South and Central Asia, has become widespread in Europe and America. For feeding its larvae, it hunts spiders, which it immobilizes with its venomous sting. Rather than digging a burrow in the ground, it gathers pieces of earth and uses its saliva to form them into long, hollow, bowl-like vessels, which it then sticks on sheltered house walls—under roofs, in attics, behind paintings, etc. The Asian mud-dauber wasp is a synanthrope, meaning it tends to live in association with humans. In human habitations, it favors places protected from the weather. The mud-dauber female inserts several paralyzed spiders into each "cup" before laying her egg in it and closing it with a mud lid. On hatching, the larvae feed on the motionless spiders. After pupation, they bite their way out of the vessel through the lid.

« *An Asian mud-dauber wasp* (Sceliphron curvatum) *with its catch, a goldenrod crab spider* (Misumena vatia).

# MUSICIANS OF THE INSECT WORLD

*Bush crickets, mole crickets, field crickets (Orthoptera), and cicadas (Hemiptera)*

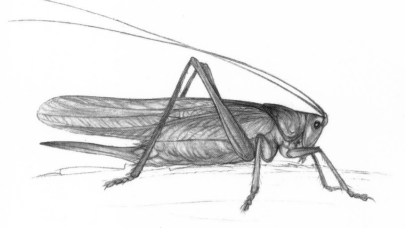

*The great green bush cricket* (Tettigonia viridissima)
*lives in Europe, Asia, and Africa*

*North American cicada of the genus* Magicicada

The longhorn beetles (Cerambycidae) produce a squeaking sound by rubbing the lower surface of its head against the grooved margin of the pronotum. Most insects make use of this way of making sound—the rubbing of two specially adapted body parts together, called stridulation. Woodboring beetles (*Ptinidae*) have another method: they make a sound like a ticking clock by tapping the head and the pronotum against the inside of the gallery they have made in old wood. When this regular sound is carried by old furniture, humans often refer to it as the "clock of death". The woodboring beetle *Hadrobregmus pertinax* uses this to attract the female.

We find the best insect musicians among orthopterans and leafhoppers (Auchenorrhyncha). Herbivorous locusts (Caelifera) can stridulate, but crickets and bush crickets (Ensifera) are better musicians still. This suborder of Orthopterans is a very old one: fossils have been dated to the Carboniferous Period, making them over 300 million years old. Ensifera differ from Caelifera in that they have long, slender antennae and are often predatory. Bush crickets stridulate through friction created by the wrinkled edges of their rigid front wings. The chirping male sends a message to his surroundings: "I'm here, and I'm looking for a partner." (The females, too, have been known to chirp.) They have their hearing organ on the tibia of forelegs. We might almost say that bush crickets hear "with their knees."

Among Ensifera, the cricket is the maestro. It, too, stridulates by producing rapid friction between transformed front wings. Unlike bush crickets, most crickets are flightless. The male of the European field cricket (*Gryllus campestris*) digs a burrow in a hot sunny place. His song comes from the mouth of the burrow on warm days and summer evenings, the aim being to attract a female to mate with. Females will lay eggs in soil near burrows, or directly into them.

The mole cricket is a strange member of the family Gryllotalpidae that lives underground. Using its scoop-shaped, extended forelegs, in the manner of a mole, it digs corridors up to one foot deep. Its scientific name, *Gryllotalpa*, is composed of *Gryllus* (the genus name of the field cricket) and *Talpa* (that of moles). The female lays eggs in underground chambers. The corridors dug by the male are especially remarkable. Although his trills can reach a volume of 90 decibels, he provides them with an amplifier in the form of a double opening on the principle of the acoustic horn or waveguide, thus providing acoustic impedance. In such an opening, the trills of the mole cricket reach 110 decibels and beyond.

The loudest sounds in the insect world are produced by cicadas, however. Cicadas are unrelated to the bush crickets (their relatives are aphids and small leafhoppers, which tap on plant stalks and stridulate at a high pitch), and they do not produce sound as orthopterans do. Cicadas stridulate by shaking membranes in the abdominal region called a tymbal, thus creating a sound of around 120 decibels that can be painful to the human ear. Cicadas often "sing" in large groups. These are so well coordinated that performers begin together; they also end together, even when interrupted. All cicadas are herbivorous and feed on sap. In some cases, their nymphs develop in the ground. Several species (notably of the South American genus *Magicicada*) are known for their extraordinarily long development—between 13 and 17 years!

« *A field cricket* (Gryllus campestris) *singing at the entrance to its burrow (above). Below is the chamber of a European mole cricket* (Gryllotalpa gryllotalpa), *in sectional view.*

# HARMFUL AND USEFUL

## *Bark beetles (Curculionidae: Scolytinae) and checkered beetles (Cleridae)*

*Larva of European red-bellied clerid*
(Thanasimus formicarius)

*North American ornate checkered beetle*
(Trichodes ornatus)

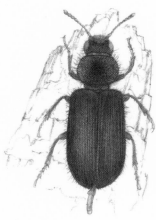

Acanthocnemus nigricans *occurs today*
*in many places around the world*

The terms "useful" and "harmful" are not really applicable in nature. Animals, plants, fungi, and microscopic organisms exist in a network of interlinked relations and are constantly adapting to their environment. Certain factors can upset this complex balance of relationships, such as the arrival of a non-native invasive species or a new disease, a sudden change in climate, or a natural disaster. Without artificial disruption to the natural environment, however, changing conditions will be managed and the balance reestablished.

"Usefulness" and "harmfulness" are human ideas by which we relate to species that destroy our crops, spread disease, or (in a better case) help in the fight against pests. Let us illustrate this with reference to forestry. In the 18th and 19th centuries, the time of Europe's Industrial Revolution, there was a great need for wood. Spruce, a solid, quick-growing tree with a straight trunk, became recognized as the ideal material for tunnel reinforcement in coal mines, the building trade, and many other purposes. In the late 18th century, many mixed forests were cut down, and their deciduous trees and evergreen trees (firs and pines) were replaced with spruce monocultures. It goes without saying that such species-poor forests are hotbeds for pests, which include the nun moth (*Lymantria monacha*) and the European spruce bark beetle (*Ips typographus*). As herbivorous insects have no natural enemies such as parasitic ichneumon wasps and insectivorous birds in field and forest monocultural environments, they multiply with ease, thus becoming—in the eyes of humans—pests. In the natural environment of the mixed forest, this would not happen. This state of affairs also impacts negatively on the spruce trees, many of which are planted in lowlands that are too hot and dry.

Bark beetles (Scolytinae) are members of the weevil family Curculionidae. Commonly, they have an interest in the trunks and branches of only one or two nutritious plants. The great spruce bark beetle (*Dendroctonus micans*) in the picture attacks pines, spruces, and sometimes larches. In coniferous woodland, it does have a notable natural enemy, the European red-bellied clerid (*Thanasimus formicarius*), whose larvae and adults attack bark beetles of all species—making it "useful" from the forester's point of view. Of course, this single natural enemy is not enough to stop bark beetles from multiplying; sadly, we are now witnessing the withering of entire forests, a state of affairs for which climate change is especially responsible.

Checkered beetles (Cleridae) are predatory. They occur in tropical regions in particular. They get their name from the colorful patterns on their pronotum and elytra. They hunt herbivorous insects on leaves, branches, tree trunks, and shrubs. Their larvae hunt the larvae of other insects in corridors under bark and galleries inside wood. An exception to this is the genus *Trichodes*, which has over 100 species in Europe, Africa, Asia, and North America. The larvae of some of these species (*T. apiarius* is a case in point) live in bees' nests, where they feed on the larvae and eggs of bees. Adults of the species fly to flowers, where they hunt other insects and also feed on pollen grains.

Relatives of the checkered beetles include *Acanthocnemus nigricans*, which is native to Australia and has infrared sensors on the underside of the thorax, by which it monitors heat radiation from forest fires. Females identify charred trees from miles away before flying to them and laying their eggs in them. Such sensors developed in the European and Asian black fire jewel beetle (*Melanophila acuminata*) in a similar way, albeit independently. The two beetles in question have similar lives. An insect's ability to adapt to extreme conditions can be truly incredible!

« *The European red-bellied clerid* (Thanasimus formicarius) *hunts the great spruce bark beetle* (Dendroctonus micans).

# THE THREAT OF FAMINE
## Locusts (Orthoptera: Caelifera)

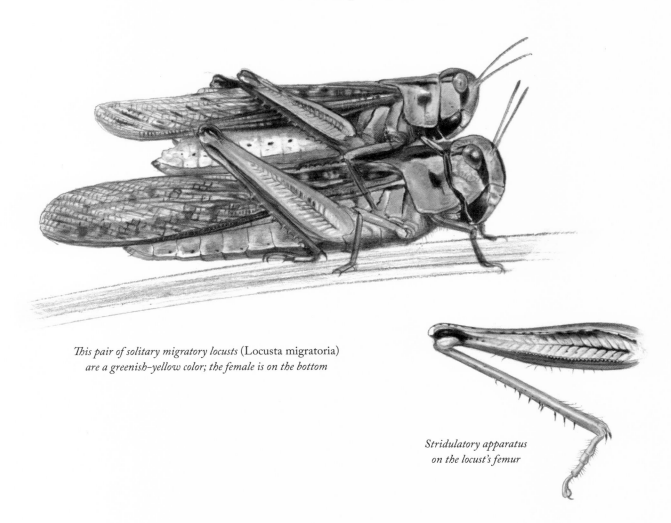

*This pair of solitary migratory locusts* (Locusta migratoria) *are a greenish-yellow color; the female is on the bottom*

*Stridulatory apparatus on the locust's femur*

The adverse effects of insect overpopulations on human civilization are described in the Bible and the Koran. Of the Ten Plagues of Egypt, four were caused by animals, and three of those were caused by insect overpopulations (bedbugs or lice, flies, and locusts). The cause of the eighth plague is the migratory locust (*Locusta migratoria*). The locusts (Caelifera) separated from the older, often predatory bush crickets (Ensifera) in the Permian Period of the late Paleozoic Era. They became more numerous in the Mesozoic Era alongside the development of terrestrial vegetation; they are exclusively herbivorous. Like Ensifera, Caelifera is an orthopteran suborder, and the two have a similar body shape. We can tell the difference between locusts by their antennae, which are not much longer than the head.

In some areas of Asia and Africa, the migratory locust is the epitome of harmful insect life, a symbol of destruction and famine. (It also lives in Europe and has been introduced to Australia and New Zealand.) In their solitary phase, adult and nymph locusts are greenish-brown in color and over 2 inches long. When population density exceeds a certain limit, they are shorter (1.5–2 inches) and yellowish-brown, and they gather in cloudlike swarms. These swarms can comprise an incredible 2 billion individuals and cover an area of over 4 square miles. In favorable conditions, with the wind behind it, a swarm of migratory locusts can fly hundreds of miles in a single day. Where the swarm settles it eats down all vegetation, which may result in famine for local human and wildlife populations.

All 10,000 locust species can jump on their hind legs. The inner side of the femur is wrinkled; the locust rubs this rapidly against the tegmina (leathery forewings), producing a chirping suggestive of meadows and steppes from spring to autumn. The stridulation is different from that of Ensifera, which chirp by moving the tegmina only. The auditory organ may be in a different position, too: while in Ensifera it is always on the tibia of the forelegs, in the locusts it may be in the abdomen. Locusts fly using a pair of hind wings. These may be strikingly colored, serving to distinguish the sexes. Some locusts have stunted wings, having lost the ability to fly.

« *A swarm of migratory locusts* (Locusta migratoria) *grazing. Migrating individuals are a yellowish-brown color.*

# LAKE AND SEA SURFACES

*Water striders (Gerridae), water measurers (Hydrometridae), water scorpions (Nepidae), diving beetles (Dytiscidae), and water scavenger beetles (Hydrophilidae)*

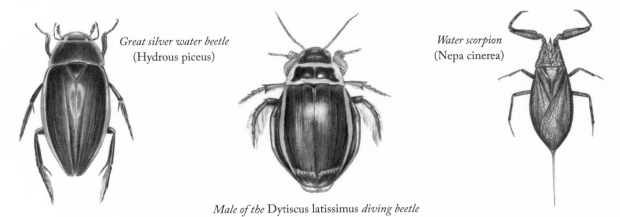

*Great silver water beetle*
(Hydrous piceus)

*Water scorpion*
(Nepa cinerea)

*Male of the* Dytiscus latissimus *diving beetle*

A few decades back, certain biologists liked to say that we live in the era of the insect. These days, such a claim leaves a bitter taste: human activity has changed earth's environment so drastically that insect numbers are shrinking at an alarming rate. The fact remains, however, that insects' incredible adaptability has allowed them to settle almost every kind of environment on our planet, from the eternal darkness of underground waters and caves, through high mountains, to freshwater lakes and temporary pools. The only environment they have not mastered in great numbers is the saltwater of the sea—although the larvae of some beetles inhabit saltwater coastal pools, and the water striders (Gerridae, of the genus *Halobates*) can move over the surface of the sea. The latter creatures live in large groups, communicate by sound signals, and move about on the sea owing to surface tension. Species of water striders that inhabit the ocean stick their eggs to pieces of solid material carried by the current.

Water striders move about surfaces of bodies of freshwater in swarms, alongside elongate insects known as water measurers (Hydrometridae). These true bugs are predatory; they use their stylet to spear and suck out small insects that fall onto the surface.

Water striders and water measurers are no strangers to us, unlike the water scorpions and other strange aquatic true bugs that live under the surface. The water scorpion *Nepa cinerea* camouflages itself in body-enveloping mud, lying in wait for crustaceans and aquatic insects, which it seizes with its forelegs and sucks in through its stiff stylet. The female lays eggs on plant stems above the surface. The male washes these with water several times to ensure that they do not dry out. The true bug *Ranatra linearis* has a similar lifestyle. Slenderer than *Nepa cinerea*, it can grow to be 1.5 inches long, making it the largest European true bug, and it tolerates saltwater. As all these aquatic bugs can fly, they may inhabit small and secluded ponds.

The rulers of stagnant waters are the large diving beetles of the family Dytiscidae and the water scavenger beetles of the family Hydrophilidae. These creatures are truly versatile: they can fly very well, live on dry land, dive in pools, even survive in groundwater. The statement at the outset of this chapter about the incredible adaptability and ability to settle almost every kind of environment applies to them in spades. Water scavenger beetles can live in compost, under rocks, in water, even in animal feces.

The predatory larvae of large diving beetles and water scavenger beetles feed on aquatic insects, tadpoles, and small fish. The larvae of the great silver water beetle (*Hydrophilus piceus*), the largest of them, grow to a length of 2.7 inches; they feed on aquatic gastropods, such as ramshorn snails and pond snails, by biting holes in their shells and using their sharp mandibles to inject digestive enzymes into the body, which they then suck out. Among the largest aquatic beetles, they are about 2 inches long. Although omnivorous, they feed mostly on plant debris. They must rise to the surface from time to time to breathe air. They do this by lifting the abdomen from the water and pumping a bubble of air under the elytra. As the spiracles of the tracheae are in the abdomen, they can breathe from this bubble for about a quarter of an hour. Diving beetles breathe in a similar way.

Although they inhabit similar environments, diving beetles and water scavenger beetles are not related. Both larvae and adults are predatory, hunting any prey within reach, principally insects and tadpoles. Large species, notably *Dytiscus marginalis* and *D. latissimus*, will try their luck with small fish, although they have so many fish enemies that they are a rarity in waters rich in fish. These beautiful creatures grow to a length of up to 1.5 inches. Sadly, they are disappearing from our world, for reasons unclear. The most likely causes are the flushing of artificial fertilizers and pesticides from fields and the unnecessary restocking of all bodies of water, including the smallest. Another possible culprit is "light smog," the ever-present lighting of human settlements and roads, which, by attracting beetles, prevents them from finding their way and seeking out partners, thus disrupting their natural way of life.

« *The aquatic true bug* Ranatra linearis *is in the foreground. By the surface is a larva of the* Dytiscus latissimus *diving beetle and two females. A larva of the great silver water beetle* (Hydrophilus piceus) *and the freshwater snail* Planorbarius *are in the center.*

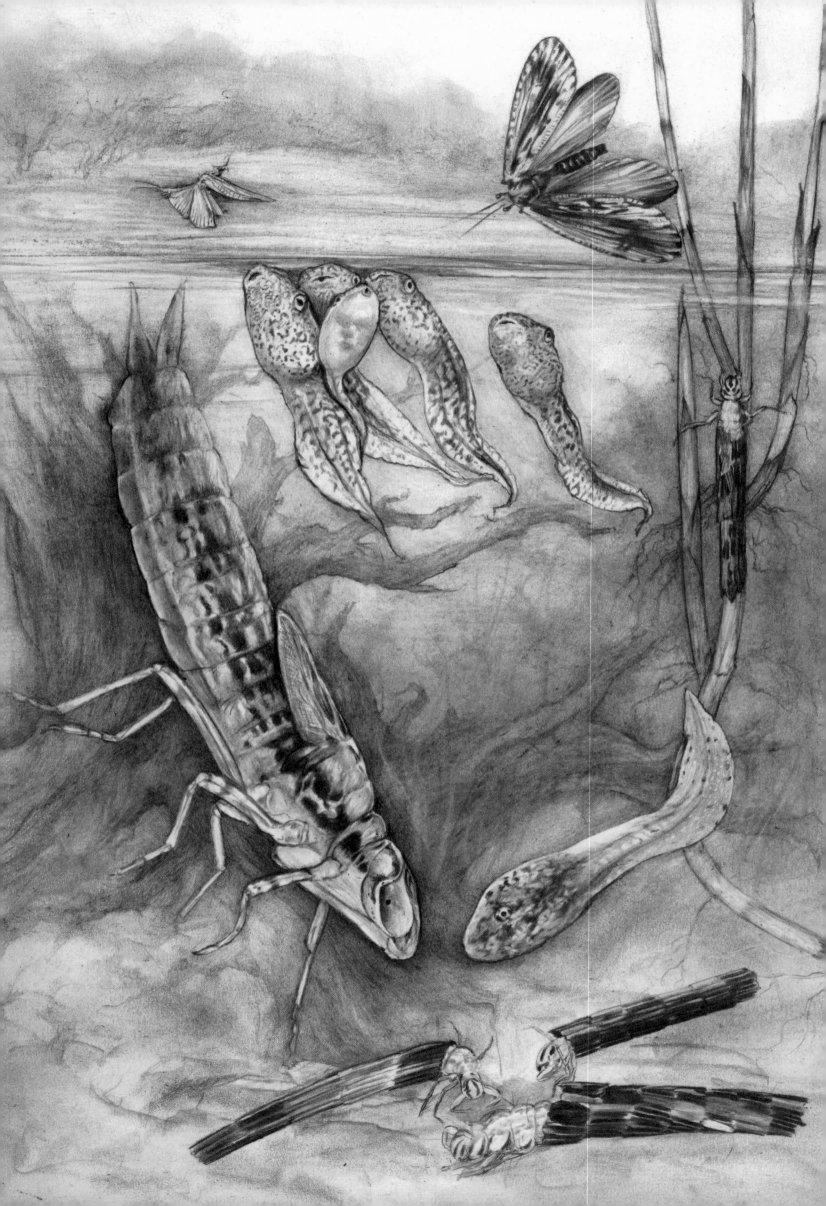

# UNDER THE SURFACES OF CLEAR POOLS

*Stoneflies (Plecoptera), dragonflies (Odonata), and caddisflies (Trichoptera)*

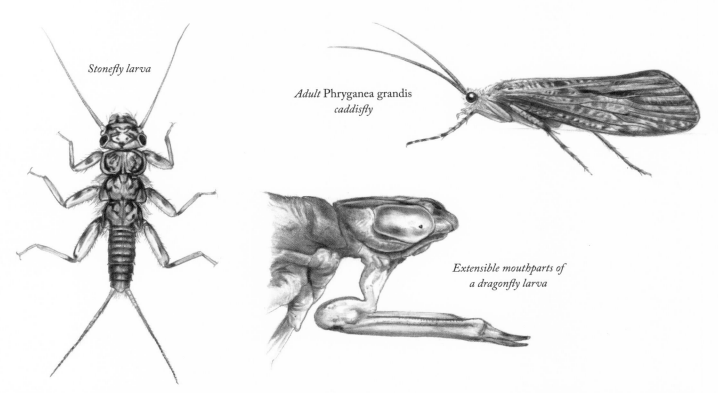

*Stonefly larva*

*Adult* Phryganea grandis *caddisfly*

*Extensible mouthparts of a dragonfly larva*

In the last chapter, we looked at large beetles and true bugs that live in the relatively warm waters of ponds and lakes with a muddy bottom and can absorb oxygen from the air above the surface. Cold mountain pools, low dams, and abandoned, rocky-bottomed quarries contain a world inhabited by other groups of insects that need clean, well-oxygenated water. Their larvae and nymphs breathe through tracheal gills; their adults fly above the water. Oxygen dissolves better in cold water, which explains why many species with gills are reliant on cold or flowing water.

By a mountain pool on a summer's day, an observer may be treated to quite a spectacle. A small, unremarkable-looking, gray-brown moth flutters around before suddenly angling its flight at the water and vanishing into it. This is a caddisfly female of the order Trichoptera, a close relative of butterflies, which has gone into the water to lay her eggs. Caddisfly larvae live underwater and are known for making a tubular case out of material they find on the bottom. For this, some species use needles from nearby trees, others shells of small gastropods or small stones. Often, the composition of a case will tell us which caddisfly species it belongs to. Rather than building a case, the larvae of some species spin a dense net to catch small aquatic creatures. The strange "cobwebs" on stones on the beds of streams are the work of caddisflies.

The caddisflies are insects that undergo a complete metamorphosis. Dragonflies, mayflies, and stoneflies undergo incomplete metamorphosis, so we refer to their larvae as nymphs. The nymphs of terrestrial insects (e.g.,

true bugs) are much like the adults, although they lack wings. The nymphs of aquatic insects bear little resemblance to the adults. Dragonfly nymphs are predators that lie in wait for their prey on the bottom or on stems of aquatic plants. Their labium has transformed into a prehensile organ, which they shoot forward to grasp prey over distances up to a third of their body length. This prey comprises mainly aquatic insects, but also tadpoles and newt larvae. Dragonfly larvae have several developmental stages. To complete their development, they go ashore and climb a reed. There, the nymph's skin bursts; out of the exoskeleton (exuvia) crawls an adult dragonfly, whose wings expand and harden in the air.

Another insect whose nymphs live mostly in cold clear water are the stoneflies (Plecoptera). Both herbivorous and carnivorous, stonefly nymphs take up to 4 years to develop. Most adult stoneflies do not feed at all (in rare cases, they feed on algae), and they live only a few days or weeks. Prior to mating, the male beats his abdomen against a base, and the female perceives the sound this makes through an auditory organ in the legs. At Lake Tahoe and Lake Baikal, we find several stonefly species that have no wings in adulthood and remain in the water their whole lives. This is most unusual, as the vast majority of aquatic insect species can leave the water. Like the mayflies, the stoneflies are a primitive insect with a very long history; fossils have dated them to the Palaeozoic Era and preserved them in the form in which they lived in swamps of the Carboniferous Period.

« *A dragonfly larva lies in wait for a tadpole. Larvae of the caddisfly* Phryganea *and a female caddisfly are just below the surface. In the background is a stonefly in flight.*

# HERDERS AND THEIR FLOCKS

*Ants (Formicidae), aphids (Aphidoidea), and ladybirds (Coccinelidae)*

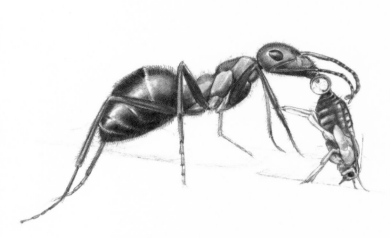

*An ant collecting honeydew from the abdomen of an aphid*

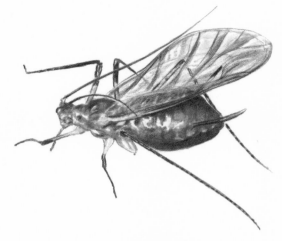

*Winged female aphid of the family* Aphididae

On rootstocks of roses and thistles and young shoots on branches of birch trees, action scenes comparable to those involving great beasts on the plains of Africa and the freezing tundra are common summer occurrences. The only significant difference is that the actors are so small as to be invisible to the human eye.

Every spring, winged female aphids hatched from hibernating eggs fly to young shoots—on trees and shrubs and mature herbaceous plants alike. The females have no need for males; they lay unfertilized eggs from which will emerge the nymphs of a wingless generation of aphids. Like the adults, these nymphs will pierce plant tissue and suck out the sap. Related to true bugs and leafhoppers, aphids are characterized by their soft, defenseless body, small size, and the great speed at which they reproduce. In the growing season, they are present in up to 40 generations! Their methods of reproduction are very various and in many cases complex. Some aphid species vacillate between asexual and sexual reproduction, giving rise to winged and wingless offspring. They lay eggs or give birth to live nymphs. They can move from one plant food to another, and they establish settled and migrating generations. Our example is one of many.

Many aphid species are myrmecophilous; this means that they use sap sucked from plants to produce honeydew in the body, which they excrete in droplets from the abdomen, thereby attracting ants, which protect the aphids in exchange for their sweet juice. And aphids have

lots of this. Rapidly reproducing aphids provide food for the larvae of hoverflies and aphid midges, lacewings, many spider species, and other arthropods. Perhaps the best-known predators of the aphid are the seven-spot ladybird (*Coccinella septempunctata*) and other ladybird (Coccinellidae) species. Ladybird larvae and adults fall on sucking aphids as though they were a banquet. It is estimated that in the course of its development a ladybird larva will eat over 600 aphids! Even so, aphid providers of honeydew are protected by ants, which do their best to drive the ladybirds away. It is sometimes said that ants "farm" and "milk" aphids. Research has recently revealed that some ant species secrete, through glands in their legs, chemicals that suppress the formation of wings in aphid nymphs. Thus do ants ensure that aphids cannot fly away.

Ladybirds give ants a hard time. First, ladybirds are protected by an armor of chitin. Second, they secrete a yellowy-orange bodily fluid between the coxae called hemolymph, which contains the toxic alkaloid coccinellin, which is strong enough to repel birds. If we press a ladybird in the palm of our hand, we can experience this hemolymph for ourselves, and we have nothing to fear from it. We should be more afraid for the ladybird itself: in recent years its species have been suppressed in their native environments by the Asian ladybeetle (*Harmonia axyridis*), artificially planted by people in many places to fight pests that attack crops.

« *Ants guarding a group of aphids attacked by a seven-spot ladybird* (Coccinella septempunctata) *and its larva (left).*

# MEAT-EATING FLIES

*Blowflies (Diptera: Calliphoridae)*

*Larva of the greenbottle fly*

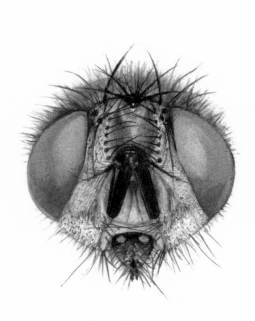

*Front view of the head of the common greenbottle fly*
(Lucilia sericata)

*Pupa of the common greenbottle fly*

Blowflies of the genus *Lucilia* are metallic green in color. They make a loud buzzing sound, spend most of their time on flowers, and feed on nectar and pollen. Female blowflies lay their eggs on meat, and it is there that their larvae develop. This meat may be the body of a live or a dead animal; in the latter case, they help with the decomposition and liquidation of the carcass.

The toadfly *Lucilia bufonivora* lays eggs in the nostrils of the common toad. It chooses a large, ideally weakened individual, or focuses on wounded areas of the toad's body. The larvae that hatch from the eggs feed on the living flesh of the toad, beginning with the nasal cavities and ending with the eyes and brain; the toad soon stops moving and eventually dies. As blowflies and toads have long been relatively abundant, attentive observers of nature asked themselves centuries ago how it could be that such dreadful parasites and such suffering were parts of God's creation. Today, we understand the developmental cycle of blowflies as the discovery of a free food niche—i.e., a source of food previously unexploited by another animal species. Notwithstanding this scientific explanation, the fact remains that a toad lying still after it has been eaten alive from the inside is a shocking sight. Incidentally, the name *Lucilia*, chosen in 1830 by French physician and entomologist Jean-Baptiste Robineau-Desvoidy, is that of the woman who murdered Roman poet and philosopher Lucretius.

Other blowflies can be considered useful creatures, as they dispose of carcasses and prevent the transmission of bacterial infections. The common greenbottle (*Lucilia sericata*) is used in modern medicine for this very purpose. Blowflies cultivated in laboratories lay eggs and sterile larvae to apply on non-healing wounds. The larvae eat dead (necrotic) tissue around wounds (e.g., long-term wounds caused by some forms of diabetes) with great accuracy, thereby cleaning and healing them; they also secrete antibacterial substances, thus disinfecting affected places. For their antibacterial secretions, the larvae are sometimes soaked in clean water, which is then used to wash a wound.

Because flies of the family Calliphoridae (not least the abundant greenbottle) are among the first life forms to find a dead body, their life cycle has been intensively studied and described by a discipline known as forensic entomology. By measuring and weighing larvae (maggots) found on a body in all their stages of development, criminal investigators can determine a victim's time of death with great accuracy.

« *A common toad* (Bufo bufo) *with its nostrils filled with larvae of the blowfly* (Lucilia bufonivora). *In the foreground is an adult blowfly.*

# FLYING LANTERNS

## Fireflies (Lampyridae) and click beetles (Elateridae)

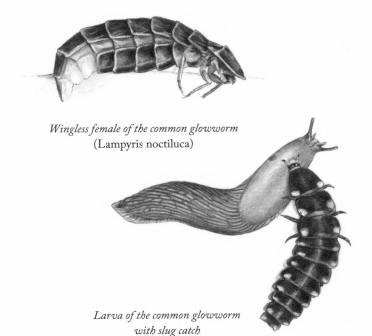

*Wingless female of the common glowworm*
(Lampyris noctiluca)

*Male of the common*
*glowworm, from below*

*South American* Pyrophorus
*click beetle—"cucojo"*

*Larva of the common glowworm*
*with slug catch*

Little lights flicker in the darkness of warm evenings in many places of the world. A common subject of folk and fairy tales, fireflies embody the miracle of nature.

Fireflies (Lampyridae) are small beetles (2.5–25 mm long) with soft elytra. They have many peculiarities. The female is often larger than the male, and in many species she is larviform, meaning she resembles her own larvae. She is wingless, and her elytra are stunted. She is distinguished from her larvae by her compound eyes (larvae have simple eyes), long antennae, and articulated feet.

The most amazing thing about fireflies is their ability to produce light: bioluminescence. Only nocturnal (nighttime) firefly species are luminescent; diurnal (daytime) species do not have this ability. The light of fireflies is the result of a complex chemical process by which, in the presence of oxygen, magnesium, and the enzyme luciferase, a substance known as luciferin produces a cold light without ultraviolet and infrared wavelengths. This light tends to be bluish-white or yellowish-orange. The male's light organ is situated at the end of the abdomen, as is that of the female, in whom light from above is not obscured by the elytra. Females of wingless firefly species commonly rest on blades of grass and herbs and leaves of bushes, where they shine their flickering light at males as an enticement to mate. They do this by emitting regular light signals that vary from species to species, enabling in-flying males to identify females of their own kind. (Sometimes fireflies of several species live in the same meadow.) Signals may vary in duration, rate of repetition, and color. Males respond to females, or vice versa, with a corresponding "Morse code" light show. As nature is full of tricks and pitfalls, however, firefly communication does not always go smoothly. Females of the large North American fireflies of the genus *Photuris* (known as the femme fatale firefly) mimic the flashing of smaller females of the genus *Photinus*. As a result, confused *Photinus* males meet not a yearned-for partner but death in the mandibles of females of a different species. This phenomenon, known as aggressive mimicry, is discussed above in the chapter on the deceptive appearance of caterpillars.

Most fireflies are predatory, although some species feed on nectar and others do not feed at all as adults. Adult fireflies live only for a few days or weeks; larvae develop over a longer period. Predatory larvae hunt insects, spiders, snails, and slugs on the ground. It is not unusual for them to attack a slug much larger than themselves. Like many other insects, firefly larvae use external digestion. Substances with which they impregnate their prey break down internal tissue, which the larva then sucks out.

The bodies of adult and larval fireflies are protected by substances they contain that are disgusting to or even toxic for predators. Larvae, too, emit light to warn insectivorous mammals and birds of their inedibility. This common natural phenomenon, known as aposematism, is discussed above in relation to butterflies, which protect themselves by Müllerian mimicry.

Genes that make up light-emitting organs are also found in related click beetles (Elateridae), some of which are indeed bioluminescent. The best-known is the South American "cucujo"—a click beetle of the genus *Pyrophorus*, which has light-emitting organs on the corners of the pronotum. It is said that the light of some cucojos is bright enough to read by!

« *A femme fatale firefly female* (Photuris; *foreground*), *a copulating pair (behind, right), and a female feeding on a smaller* Photinus *male.*

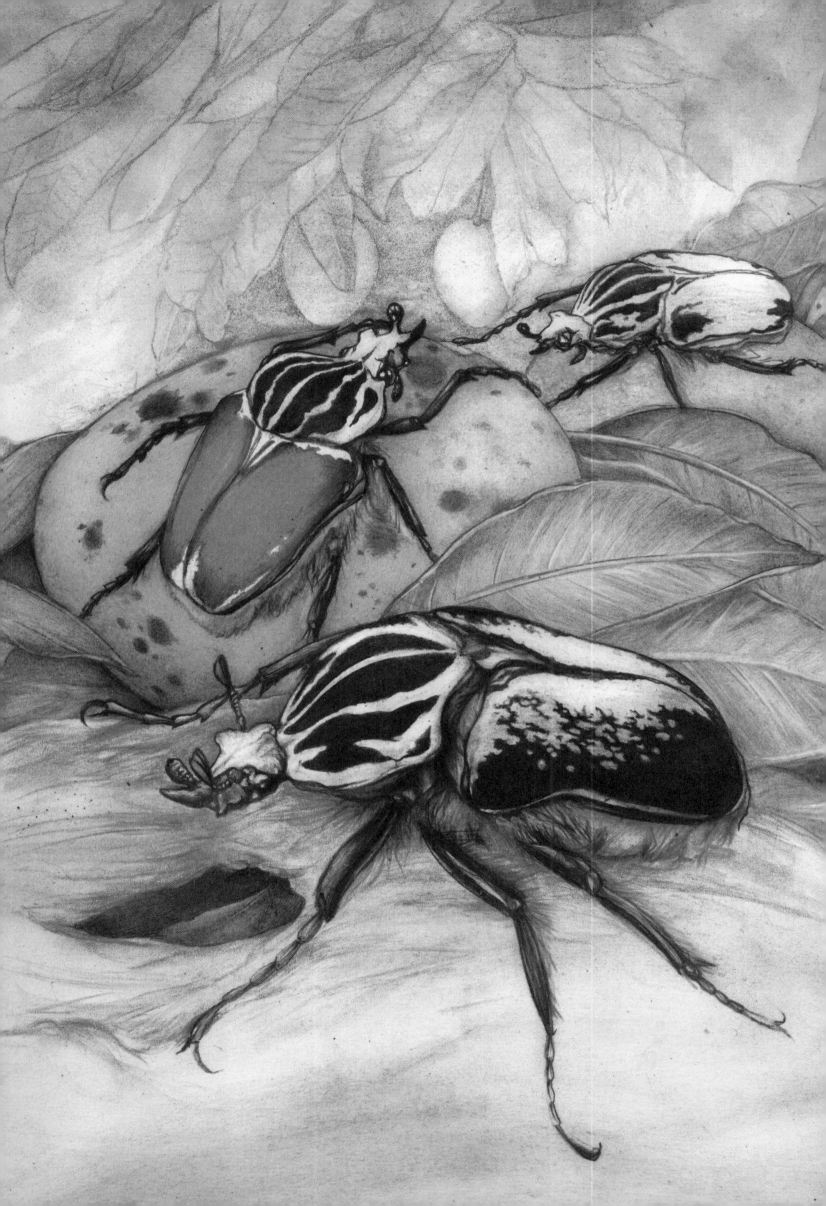

# BEETLE GOLIATHS

## *Flower chafers (Coleoptera: Scarabaeidae: Cetoniinae)*

*Huge larva of the genus* Goliathus

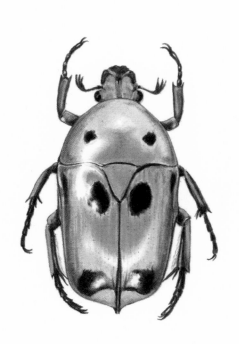

Heterorrhina sexmaculata
*flower chafer from tropical Asia*

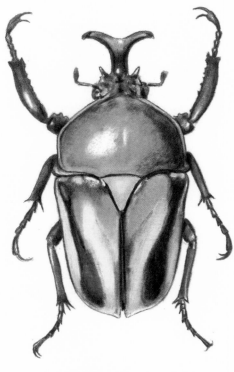

*Male of African flower chafer*
Eudicella gralli

Imagine yourself driving along a road in equatorial Africa. There is a sudden bang. The windscreen is shattered, so you stop the car at the side of the road. You have just encountered one of six species of the genus *Goliathus*, the largest beetles in Africa and one of the largest insects altogether. The Goliath beetle takes its name from the gigantic warrior in the Bible who was killed by a slingshot from the much smaller David.

The Goliath beetles are flower chafers. Like a buzzing, flying gemstone, they travel from one nectar-rich flower to the next. Flower chafers live all over the world, in over 4,000 species. Most of them have pastel or metallic coloration, and some have remarkable horns on their heads. Close relatives of the scarab beetles, the flower chafers have a robust body and reinforced elytra. Even so, they are excellent flyers. They have one notable curiosity: elytra that are convex at the sides. By lifting them slightly on takeoff, an aperture is created between the elytra and the thorax from which the wings emerge; the flower chafer flies with the elytra closed. On landing, it lifts the elytra slightly and folds the wings beneath them.

As no flower is strong enough to bear the 100 grams of the Goliath beetle, and as it needs food high in energy, it likes to feed on overripe fruit and tree sap. Goliath beetle males can be over 4 inches long (females are smaller), which is nothing compared to the larvae, which are up to 10 inches long and weigh 3.5 ounces! Although Goliaths are popular with beetle collectors, not much is known about how their larvae live in the wild. Probably they live in litter in primeval forests, feeding on plant debris (like other flower chafers) and insect eggs and larvae. To grow, they need far more protein than their smaller relatives. Goliath beetles are also kept in insectaria, where larvae are bred successfully in a mix of rotting wood and leaf litter, with cat or dog food pellets for extra nutrition. After several months of growth, a mature larva forms the solid cocoon in which it pupates, from soil. In the wild, it passes the dry season in the cocoon; when the rain comes, it leaves the softened cocoon as an adult.

All species of Goliath beetles have vertical stripes on the pronotum, and lusterless, velvety elytra. The males are larger than the females, with a Y-shaped horn at the front of the head for use in combat with other males over food and partners. The females lack this horn; the front of their head is wedge-shaped and their front tibias are spined—features that assist their burrowing for when they lay eggs.

« *African Goliath beetles feasting on overripe fruit.* Goliathus regius *is front and back;* Goliathus goliatus *is in the center.*

# TITANS OF THE RAINFOREST GLOOM

*Longhorn beetles (Cerambycidae) and rhinoceros beetles (Scarabaeidae)*

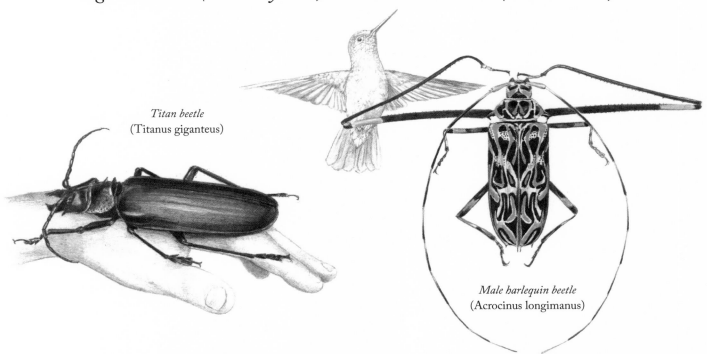

*Titan beetle*
(Titanus giganteus)

*Male harlequin beetle*
(Acrocinus longimanus)

For this chapter, we will stay with the giants of the insect world. We will move from Africa to the tropical rainforests of South America, home to our planet's largest beetles. Having said that, whichever one is truly the largest depends on one's point of view. So let us look at a few contenders.

The rhinoceros beetle, known as the Hercules (*Dynastes hercules*), is a member of the scarab family (Scarabaeidae), where we also find cockchafers, flower chafers, and various maybeetles. Including all its outgrowths, it has the longest body of all beetles, perhaps all flying insects. From his pronotum the male grows a long, stationary horn, which touches against a toothed, movable horn that grows from below. The body alone is 3.5 inches long; with the horn, that length can double to 7 inches! The female has no such horn on either the pronotum or the head, making her much shorter. The male uses his horns in combat for mating rights to a female, the aim being to grasp his rival in the tweezer-like grip of his horns before tossing him away. It is said that a Hercules beetle is so strong that it can lift an object a whopping 850 times heavier than itself! When in danger, it tries to scare away predators with a loud huffing sound, made by friction between the abdomen and the elytra. While adults prefer to feed on sweet, overripe fruit, their huge larvae live in rotting wood, thus helping the decomposition of dead trees and the recycling of nutrients, which pass into the soil. The Hercules beetle lives in an area from southern Mexico down to Bolivia and is also widespread on several islands of the Lesser Antilles in the Caribbean. The genus *Dynastes* comprises six similar species that also occur in the tropical Americas.

The titan beetle (*Titanus giganteus*) is believed to be the very largest beetle. The longest documented specimen measured 6.6 inches long, not counting horns, other

outgrowths, or antennae. Titans are mostly nocturnal and attracted by light. The titan, too, has a lifestyle that binds it to the rotting wood of great trees of the primeval forest, although as yet we know little about the behavior of its larvae. It is commonly found on the edge of a clearing in the Amazonian rainforest. The history of sightings of this enormous longhorn beetle is a fascinating, adventurous one. The first mention of the titan beetle is from 1765, in an illustrated encyclopedia with a drawing by French naturalist Louis Jean-Marie Daubenton. Thanks to this drawing, Carl Linnaeus, the founder of zoological and botanical nomenclature, came up with the scientific name *Titanus giganteus* to describe the species. The actual specimen seen by Daubenton was lost, however, and over 150 years passed before the titan was next spotted by a scientist. The finder was a German orchid enthusiast named Wörner, the place a fish's stomach by the Rio Negro. Wörner took the beetle's remains back to Europe, thereby making a name for himself. Collectors offered him great sums of money for the remains, causing him to return to Brazil to collect more of the drowned beetles. When he next arrived in Europe, collectors sailed out of the port to meet him.

There are many more enormous longhorn beetles. Some would say that the titan and the Hercules are surpassed in size by the magnificent sabertooth longhorn beetle (*Macrodontia cervicornis*) from the Amazonian rainforests, although several centimetres of its length are accounted for by the toothed mandibles that project from its front. Another remarkable American beetle is the brightly colored harlequin longhorn (*Acrocinus longimanus*), which occurs from southern Mexico down to Uruguay. Its body length can exceed 2.5 inches, with another 2.5–4 inches accounted for by its extremely long forelegs.

« *A pair of Central American rhinoceros beetles of the species* Hercules (Dynastes hercules). *As she has no horn on her pronotum, the female is smaller.*

# MY HOME IS MY CASTLE

*Fig wasps (Chalcidoidea), gall wasps (Cynipidae), and sawflies (Tenthredinidae)*

*Gall wasp*
(Cynips quercusfolii)

*Willow gall sawfly*
(Pontania proxima)

*Rose bedeguar gall*
(Diplolepis rosae)

Things happen in nature by a complex interplay of relations among animals and plants, and sometimes this web gets a bit tangled. Let us consider the tiny wasps of the superfamily Chalcidoidea, whose life is bound up with that of the fig—just as the great Greek philosopher and naturalist Aristotle suspected over 2,000 years ago.

Figs (*Ficus*) are trees and shrubs, some of which are familiar to us as pot plants. Other species are cultivated for their tasty fruit, and all serve as food for monkeys, fruit bats, and many different birds. There are about 800 species of fig in the world. They are characterized by a unique spherical inflorescence (i.e., flower head), which contains tiny flowers and seeds. Known as the syconium, the succulent inflorescence is in fact an extension of the stalk. The pollination of all fig trees and shrubs is dependent on small fig wasps of the family Agaonidae, which are chalcidoids. Figs and chalcidoids have developed in tandem for between 70 and 90 million years, in a coevolution beneficial to all. The tiny flowers in the fig's syconium are hermaphrodite (short-styled), female (long-styled), or sterile. The front part of the syconium is the ostiole, a small opening by which the wasp enters the plant. When the wasp finds a hermaphrodite or sterile flower, it lays its eggs and then dies. Tiny larvae develop inside the fig. The first of these to emerge are wingless, often blind males. They bite holes in the fig and fertilize the female wasps that emerge after them. The fertilized females, covered in pollen, fly out through the holes and go off in search of another fig. With the help of the wind, they distribute the pollen over dozens of miles. Having found a new syconium, they pollinate the flower inside. If this flower is hermaphrodite, the whole cycle is repeated. If the fig contains only long-styled female flowers, the wasp pollinates them but cannot lay her eggs inside; she then dies. The fig absorbs the body of the dead wasp and her eggs and produces seeds and a sweet fruit. These female figs are the sweet fruit we eat in fresh or dried form.

Every species of fig has its own species of fig wasp, to which it provides refuge in exchange for pollination. To ensure that the right species of wasp with the right pollen enters the syconium, and that wasps bringing pollen from other figs are barred, the ostiole should be the same size as the right wasp's body. This is not always the case, however: some figs can be pollinated by more than one wasp species.

To make matters more complicated still, relatives of chalcidoids of the Pteromalidae family do not pollinate figs. As parasitoids, they are interested in pollinating fig wasps, not figs. Certain non-pollinating species of chalcidoid focus on certain species of fig to deliver them to certain pollinating species of chalcidoid. The genus Apocrypta mainly parasitizes the pollinating genus *Ceratosolen*, for instance. In the picture, *Apocrypta guineensis* is thrusting its long, S-shaped ovipositor into the syconium of a Cape fig (*Ficus sur*), which is found over a wide area of tropical Africa. Somewhere inside the fig are the larvae of pollinating wasps, on which the *Apocrypta* larvae will feed.

« *The fig wasp* Apocrypta guineensis *lays its eggs on the fruit of the fig* Ficus sur.

# SOME LIKE IT COLD

*Snow flies (Limoniidae), snow fleas (Boreidae), and springtails (Collembola)*

*Group of* Isotoma saltans *glacier fleas on snow*

Isotoma saltans *glacier flea (detail)*

On the ocean, in a dark cave, under a foaming mass of water, we find insects practically everywhere. Although it is hard to believe, insects live on snow too.

Many dipterans and beetles are active on humid, relatively warm days in late autumn and winter. Some beetles that live under bark and in arboreal fungi reproduce in winter (their larvae develop in spring and summer), limiting their activity to days when the temperature is above freezing, ideally 40–50°F.

Some insects are in their element in the cold season. They may have to put up with bad weather, but they have fewer predators and parasites to contend with than on warmer days. Dipteran limoniid crane flies are widespread in the Arctic and Antarctic. They include the snow fly genus *Chionea*, strange wingless creatures with sweet thick glycerol in their hemolymph to keep them from freezing. From what we know from several of the 40 *Chionea* species, its larvae live under a surface layer of dead plants, feeding on organic debris, including the feces of small rodents. Adult snow flies move slowly about snow fields and the mouths of caves. They are not known to feed. They have been observed at temperatures between 20–30°F, although experiments suggest that they can survive below 14°F.

Although the snow fleas (genus *Boreus*) are from a completely different insect group, they are similar in appearance to snow flies. They, too, have long legs and no wings. They belong to the scorpionflies (Mecoptera), a small order of insects related to the fleas. Most scorpionflies have trans-

lucent wings with numerous cross-veins, long mandibles, and small pincers on the abdomen. Snow fleas do not fly and have small bristles instead of wings. They, too, place their larvae in fallen leaves and moss. Adult snow fleas seek out mating partners in the snow. During copulation, the female is on top, which is exceptional among insects, indeed animals as a whole. Although they move slowly, they can jump. Athletes often encounter snow fleas in wooded mountains: they tend to appear on cross-country ski trails.

Winter's end sometimes presents us with a strange phenomenon: snow layered in tiny dark dots. A closer look reveals that the dots are alive and jumping. They are springtails (Collembola), which are no longer considered insects, although they are close relatives. All springtails are small, wingless, and able to jump by snapping an abdominal appendage, which is folded beneath the body. They live in soil and leaf litter. Due to their abundance, they are very important for the decomposition of organic matter and the formation of humus. While several springtail species are agricultural pests, others are helpful to crops by destroying fungal diseases in plants. The behavior of a springtail species known as the glacier flea (*Isotoma saltans*) is truly extraordinary. At winter's end, glacier fleas occur en masse in old snow, where they feed on algae, pollen, plant debris, and microorganisms living in wind-blown dust. The huge number of these tiny bouncing dots in the snow is difficult to believe: up to 1,000 in a single square foot, i.e. 100 million of them in one hectare of forest!

« *Snow fleas* (Boreus hyemalis) *copulating in the snow. Unlike with other insects, the female is on top.*

# THE LOVED AND THE UNLOVED

## *Earwigs (Dermaptera)*

*Southeast Asian earwig* (Apachyus) *with outspread wings*

*Pincers on the abdomen of an earwig (detail)*

Some species and groups of insects are so popular with us that we have made them into characters in children's stories, films, and games. These popular insects have in common bright colors and rounded shapes, and they do not have sharp mandibles or spikes. We associate some insects with industriousness or self-sacrifice for the good of the community. Such association of animals with human qualities is known as anthropomorphism. The seven-spot ladybird, with its red elytra and charming black spots, is a good example of an insect with an appealing appearance. For this, we forgive it the toxic yellow liquid that gushes from all its joints, its occasional attempts to bite us, and its ruthlessness as a hunter of aphids. The beautifully colored butterfly is another charmer. The sight of it flying from flower to flower on a summer's day lifts our hearts. Although in stories, butterflies tend to represent changeability and superficiality, this is at least better than symbolizing nightmares and death, as is the case with certain moths. Social insects, too, are popular with humans—especially those that make honey, such as the bee—or are slow, round, and furry like the bumblebee. The wasp comes out of the human reckoning much worse, even though its sting is less dangerous than the bee's. Perhaps people see its striking yellow and black coloration as a warning of danger, even where the species in question is harmless. Besides, the diligence of bees and the industriousness of ants are proverbial.

Other insects unpopular with humans include mosquitoes (buzzing and biting), flies (annoying), wasps (aggressive), fleas (biting)—basically all those who share our world that can get on our nerves. In some cases, distaste for an insect is justified—if it spreads a virulent disease or causes plague and famine, for instance. Often, however, our fear and distaste are directed at innocent, harmless species whose bad reputation is due to superstition and ignorance.

The least popular insects include the whole of the order Dermaptera. In many languages, their common name is derived from the word for "ear". Hence they are known as "earwigs" in English, "perce-oreilles" in French, "Ohrwürmer" in German, and "ušáci" in Czech. How did they come by this name? Well, it may be because of the shape of their wings, which do indeed look rather like human ears. As earwigs are reluctant flyers, the sight of them with wings outspread is rare. There is a widespread belief that earwigs climb into the ears of human sleepers, which is untrue, as they have no reason to.

But the earwig is indeed a nocturnal creature. It spends the day in darkness or under a pile of logs or decomposing plants. At night, it climbs about looking for food; some species feed on animal matter, others on plants.

Earwigs have striking pincers on their abdomen. These movable forceps can be used for self-defense, the grasping of prey (some species are predatory), the holding of a partner during copulation, and the folding of their wings under their short, leathery elytra.

Earwigs undergo incomplete metamorphosis. The recently hatched nymph resembles the adult in shape, although its body is without pigment, so it's pale. As the nymph matures, its body darkens gradually, in most cases from the abdomen toward the head. The female earwig digs an oval-shaped hole in which to lay her cluster of eggs. She stays with her eggs, protecting them from predators and ridding them of mold, as the place tends to be humid. She also helps her tiny nymphs exit the eggs, the remnants of which will serve as their first food. Before their first moult, nymphs live with the mother, who feeds them on food she has regurgitated, after the fashion of many birds.

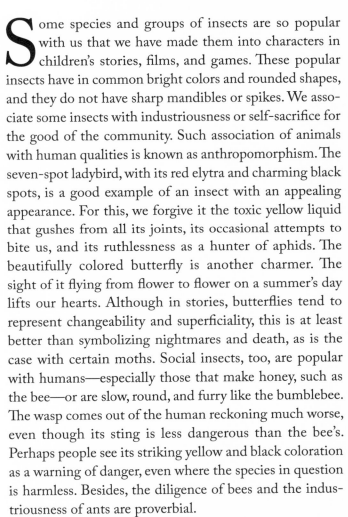

« *A female common earwig* (Forficula auricularia) *watches over her eggs. Behind her, two earwigs are copulating, clinging together by their pincers.*

# A LIFE IN HAIR

## *Fleas (Siphonaptera), lice (Anoplura), and louse flies (Hippoboscidae)*

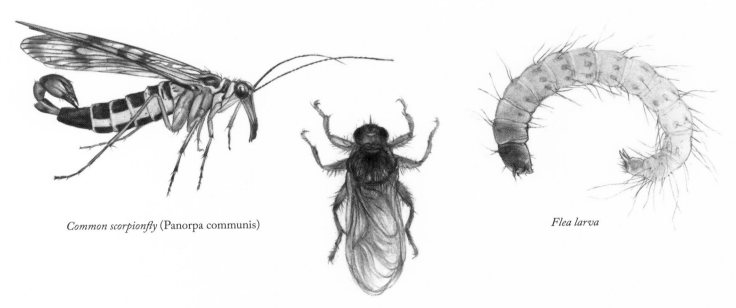

*Common scorpionfly* (Panorpa communis)

*Flea larva*

*Winged deer fly* (Lipoptena cervi)

Most if not all animal parasites have one characteristic in common: great simplicity of body form goes hand in hand with reduced dimensions as well as adaptation to extreme conditions on (with ectoparasites) or inside (with endoparasites) the body of the host. The first insects appeared over 350 million years ago, between the Devonian and Carboniferous Periods, and they were not parasites. Nor were there insect parasites 100 million years later, in the Permian Period. The earliest fossil evidence we have of insect parasites is from the Mesozoic Era. Most insect parasites developed in large insect orders that are still with us today, notably hymenopterans and dipterans. (Above, we discuss some of these, e.g., saber wasps and greenbottles.) In these families, however, only the larvae are parasitical; adults differ in no way from their non-parasite relatives. Let us now look at a few insect groups that remain with a host their whole lives.

Louse flies (Lipoptena) are dipterans with large claws and a flat body shape. They descend on their hosts—which are mostly ungulates—from trees and shrubs. No sooner has a louse fly landed on a deer than it loses its wings and begins to suck blood. The larva grows inside the female by forming a prepupa, which the mother releases to the ground, where the pupa develops.

The louse fly's appearance tells us that it is a dipteran, at least while it still has its wings. Fleas and lice, however, are so well adapted to life in the fur or feathers of warm-blooded animals that their origin was long a mystery. We had to wait for genetic analysis to show us that wingless, "flattened-sideways" fleas of the order Siphonaptera evolved from scorpionflies (Mecoptera). While larvae feed on organic debris separated from the host, adult fleas spend their whole life sucking blood attached to the host or in its nest. They lack eyes, but their legs have strong claws capable of clinging to fur and feathers. Fleas are significant vectors of dangerous bacterial disease, such as plague and typhus, which they transfer to humans from rodents. Fleas are also intermediate hosts of some species of tapeworms. Relatively recently, fossils were discovered of enormous fleas with remnants of wings—fleas that probably sucked the blood of feathered dinosaurs and pterosaurs. Between 6 and 9 inches long, these Jurassic and Cretaceous fleas are a great example of evolution from free-flying scorpionfly to wingless, half-blind, sedentary parasite.

Scientists were long clueless about the order of winged insects from or within which the slow, wingless, parasitical louse (Phthiraptera or Anoplura) evolved. This turned out to be the booklice (Psocodea), which we may encounter in the pages of books. Not big on reading, booklice like to feed on the glue used in bookbinding. Phthiraptera and Psocodea are not much alike: the former is flat on top with legs with a single large claw on the end. The legs bend together for the claw to hook into fur or feathers. Unlike fleas, lice undergo incomplete metamorphosis; their larvae (nymphs) develop in the fur or feathers of the host, along with the adults. There are about 500 species of lice, almost all of which are bound to a single host species. One such host are people, who attract two species: the human louse (previously known as the "body louse" and the "head louse") and the pubic louse. Lice, too, suck blood and can transmit disease including typhus; fortunately, though, they tend to cause only itching. Delousing treatments are effective against louse eggs, known as nits, as is the shaving of an affected area.

« *The sucking louse* (Linognathus setosus; *left*) *and the dog flea* (Ctenocephalides canis; *back and right*) *in a dog's coat.*

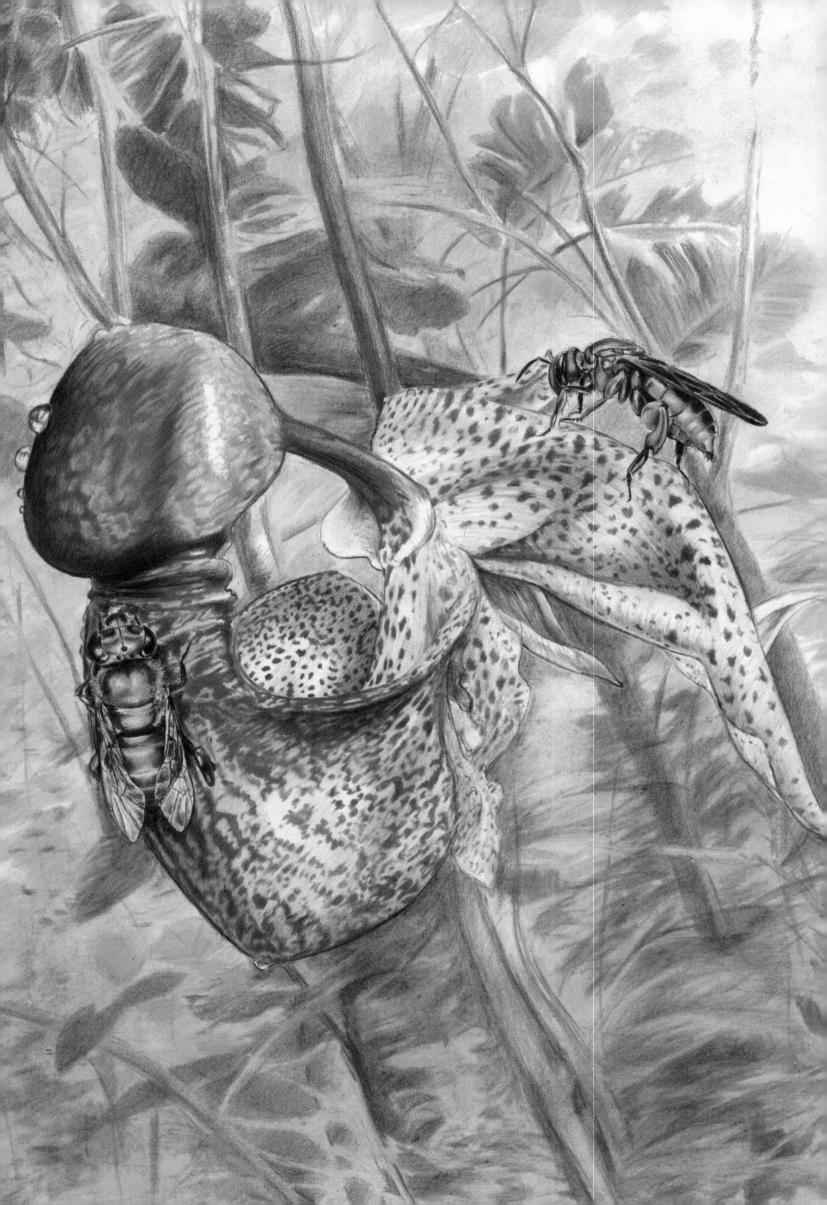

# CHEATING ORCHIDS
## Bees and wasps (Hymenoptera: Apoidea, Vespoidea)

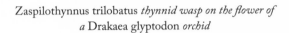

Zaspilothynnus trilobatus *thynnid wasp on the flower of a* Drakaea glyptodon *orchid*

Exaerete dentata *bee from Bolivia*

In 1862, Charles Darwin wrote a book entitled *Fertilisation of Orchids*. Above, we discuss the co-evolution of figs and fig wasps, as we do an "arms race" in the chapter on mimicry. The sophisticated orchid plants evolve by manipulating their pollinators, sometimes to the extent of cheating them. The lower part of the late spider orchid (*Ophrys holoserica*) resembles female bees (*Eucera*) and bumblebees (*Tetralonia*), thereby confusing males into an attempt to copulate with the flower by which the orchid is pollinated. This is about more than the similarity seen by the human eye: a bee's eye perceives other parts of the ultraviolet light spectrum, and it is of this that the orchid takes advantage. The bee sees a far more faithful represent-ation than we might imagine—e.g., it sees the white petals of the daisy as blue and the yellow globeflower as pink. Orchids can even attract pollinating males by mimicking the female scent. This has nothing to do with coevolution or trade; it is a straightforward deception—the bee receives not a single drop of nectar for the act of pollination.

Orchids of the genus *Brassia* mimic spiders. The female wasps by which they are pollinated hunt spiders, immobilizing them with their sting, as described in an earlier chapter. On seeing an orchid flower shaped like a spider, the confused wasp jabs it with its sting, releasing a load of pollen on itself. It then passes this pollen on to the next orchid on its round.

The Australian orchid *Drakaea glyptodon* is pollinated by the thynnid wasp *Zaspilothynnus trilobatus*. Not only does its flower resemble the female wasp, but it also has a joint by which it moves like a hammer when the deceived male attempts to copulate with it, releasing a pollen shower on the male on the other side of the flower. Even so, the male is not discouraged; he moves on to the next flower, where he passes on his pollen.

Orchids of the genus *Coryanthes* opt for a different strategy. They cannot provide the pollinator with nectar, for they do not even produce it. Instead, they provide it with a scent. It is common for a female insect to release fragrant pheromones particular to her species, thereby attracting males over several miles.

Owlet moths are particularly well known for this, as their males have highly sensitive feathery antennae. As for the small bee of the genus *Euglossina*, the male has the scent, not the female. He collects scents from all over the forest in small "tanks" on his hind legs. Depending on the species, *Euglossina* gather scents of rotting wood, various flowers, even feces. Flowers of the orchid *Coryanthes* hold the basic substance of fragrances mixed by the *Euglossina* male from various sources. By this unique, self-mixed scent, the male attracts a mate. The orchid exploits the bee's weakness for its scent by preparing a trap in the form of a lipped container of fluid. While collecting the fragrant substance within, the male falls into the container. Knobs on the walls of the container guide the male to the exit along a spout. On reaching the opening, he must pass through a set of jaws. Pollinia attach to his back as he forces his way out at last. In his quest for scent, he then hurries on to the next flower, where the entire process is repeated, ending with his fertilizing of the orchid's stigma with the pollen on his back.

« *The* Euglossina *bee gathers scents on* Coryanthes *orchid flowers in the rainforests of South America.*

# SCOURGE OF NORTH AND SOUTH
## Mosquitoes (Diptera: Culicidae)

*Larva of the yellow fever mosquito*
(Aedes aegypti)

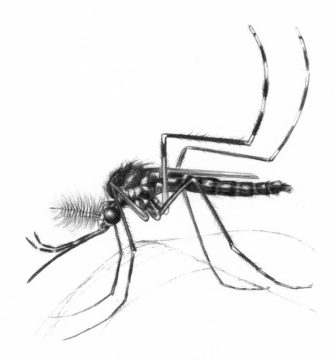

*Male of the yellow fever mosquito* (Aedes aegypti),
*with feathery antennae*

osquitoes are a scourge in all lands with an abundance of stagnant water, swamps, ponds, tributaries of lower reaches of rivers, even ordinary shallow pools. In late spring, as the snow of the tundra around the Arctic Circle thaws, swarms of mosquitoes rise from the lakes remaining on the flat landscape. These mosquitoes are of several species, the most numerous being *Aedes nigripes*. Although they are not vectors of viral infection, their huge numbers and bloodthirsty habits force whole herds of reindeer to migrate northwards.

The further south we travel, the likelier that we will encounter a disease-carrying mosquito. Mosquitoes of the genus *Culex* live in middle latitudes with a mild climate. Fertilized females of the common house mosquito (*Culex pipiens*) wait out the winter in damp underground spaces. In early spring, they lay their eggs in shallow pools and ponds. Larvae live in water, feeding on microorganisms and organic matter and breathing surface air through a siphon on the abdomen. *Culex* may transmit encephalitis and other viral diseases. A greater menace, however, is represented by the mosquito genera *Aedes* and *Anopheles*, which are widespread throughout the tropics and subtropics, except, of course, in the arid desert.

The best-known species of the genus *Aedes* is the yellow fever mosquito (*A. aegypti*), which originated in Africa but is now found all over the world. Like others of its genus, it has white markings on its legs and the sides of its abdomen. It is responsible for the spread of yellow fever,

the Zika virus, dengue fever, and other dangerous illnesses. Its larvae can live in vases, discarded bottles, and uncovered barrels. Disposal sites for old tires are a particular danger: larvae hatch by the thousand in their water-filled rims.

Mosquitoes of the genus *Anopheles* are transmitters of malaria. They are easily distinguished from other mosquitoes by the fact that when at rest their hind legs and abdomen stick up in the air rather than sitting parallel to the ground. Anopheles larvae keep to stagnant waters. From hatching, it takes 5 to 14 days for larvae to develop into adults, which explains the ease of their survival in temporary pools. As with all mosquitoes, only the female bites and sucks blood, which she needs for the maturation of her eggs. Males live for a few days only, during which they feed on the nectar of flowers. We recognize the male by the more striking feathering of his antennae.

As for basic natural protection against the bite of an *Anopheles* or *Aedes* mosquito, both genera avoid direct sunlight, seek out shady, damp, windless places, and are at their most active between evening and early morning. They are naturally attracted by the evaporation of carbon dioxide from human skin, as well as aftershaves, perfumes, creams, and deodorants. As protection against them, people are advised to wear long sleeves and long pants in the evening, ideally in lighter colors. For nighttime protection, a mosquito net should be used so that it is not disturbed during sleep. Also, containers such as watering cans and vases should be regularly drained or have their water changed.

« *The blood-sucking female of the yellow fever mosquito* (Aedes aegypti) *can transmit several dangerous illnesses to people.*

The author of this book is leading
Czech entomologist Jiří Kolibáč,
head of the Department of Entomology
at the Moravian Museum in Brno.
This work is based on his lifelong research
and observations.

For more info, check out the following websites:

www.insectidentification.org
www.inaturalist.org
bugguide.net
www.si.edu/spotlight/buginfo

© B4U Publishing for Albatros,
an imprint of Albatros Media Group, 2023
5. května 1746/22, Prague 4, Czech Republic
Author: Jiří Kolibáč
Illustrators: Pavla Dvorská & Pavel Dvorský
Translator: Andrew Oakland
Editor: Scott Alexander Jones

Printed in China by Leo Paper Group